# STREAMS
# OF
# LIFE

Ambassador

STREAMS OF LIFE
First Published 1988 Copyright © 1988 Eric Stewart
ISBN 0 907927 29 7

Ambassador Productions Ltd.
Providence House
Hillview Avenue
Belfast BT5 6JR

Printed in the United Kingdom by Ambassador Productions Ltd.

# INDEX

## ACKNOWLEDGEMENTS

My sincere thanks is expressed to many authors whose works were consulted in this publication. Also to Rev. Douglas Crossman for writing the foreword. In particular I wish to thank Mrs. Eveline Bell for her excellent work in typing and correcting the manuscript and to my wife for proof-reading the same. I was also greatly encouraged and guided by Mr. Sam Lowry in the entire publication procedure.

## DEDICATION

To my wife, Yvonne and family who have been a constant inspiration in the Lord's service.

## ANNIVERSARY

The publication of this book coincides with the two hundred and fiftieth anniversary of the conversions of John and Charles Wesley, and the twentieth anniversary of full-time Christian service by the author.

# FOREWORD

What do most of us look for when we read a Biography? - We want to be informed by the facts of the life in question - we want these to be accurate and interesting. Also, we surely want the life that's written about to live we want a real honest depiction of the character - like Cromwell, we want him "warts and all," yet no caricature. But we also need to have that life, especially if it is a Christian one, to challenge and stimulate us to a higher state of grace for ourselves.

So many of the lives of Wesley have failed to satisfy these criteria. Some are excellent for their historical and social comments of the age, but missed the whole wonder and glory of the spiritual experience they were dealing with. Some have grasped the heart of the Wesley experience but were void in their placing of the social and spiritual background. Some seemed so unsympathetic to the experience of the Holy Spirit in Wesley's life, and the interpretation he himself gave it.

In this excellent biography, I believe you have a blend of all these essentials. The times in which Wesley lived are given so graphically and interestingly that I believe many who read it will understand for the first time something of the appalling nature of the society in which the great Awakener moved.

Then we are given the life and spiritual experienes of a man who may well have been the greatest warrior for God since the Apostle Paul. The writer understands what Wesley was writing about when he related the heart-warming experience of May 24, 1738, and the enduement of the spirit which came at Fetter's Lane on January 1, 1739. He can do so because he himself has been open to the workings of the Spirit both in "heart warming" and the enduing.

I have seen the life of the author pass through the stages of being an itinerant evangelist as a young man with the Faith Mission to being a church planter and builder of a strong fellowship in the Bangor Independent Methodist Church, which fellowship of churches he helped to found. Now I see him as a clear thinking, deeply informed lecturer and theologian as principal of the Independent Methodist Bible College in Portrush, Northern Ireland. Not too often do we see such an astonishing and encouraging changing of life from farm boy to College Principal. I commend this book. I'm glad he's written it. I hope you'll read it. I wish a better hand than mine had writen the foreword.

Yours in the Grace of our Lord Jesus Christ,


Douglas A. Crossman, Michigan U.S.A.

# INTRODUCTION

The passing of time places a critical test upon the value of any man's labours. The storms of life have eroded the hardest surfaces, and buried civilizations in twentieth century living. Men, even famous men, have their little day and pass away. They are soon forgotten as others step into the breach.

There are, however, exceptions to the rule. When God raises up men for crucial times in history, their influence reaches to eternity. John Wesley was just one of those who was so ordained for the eighteenth century. Two hundred and fifty years after his conversion to Christ, he is revered by the people of God throughout the world.

If Wesley were to return he would probably be quite surprised to find how honoured he has become. He did not go forth to acquire fame.

There was no pursuit of self glory. God's time to favour England with a spiritual revival had arrived. The Wesley brothers along with George Whitefield, and others were the human channels through which He would pour His divine life and power. In humble consecration and utter abandonment to the great Saviour they had found, they went everywhere declaring the gospel of redeeming grace. Doors opened on every hand and life swept through the valley or moral and spiritual death.

Nevertheless this union of divine sovereignty and human responsibility has immortalised Wesley and his ministry in the hearts of millions around the world. The predominance of Wesley is in consequence of the strategy which attended his evangelistic labours.

It was he who effected the longest and most active ministry. In addition, the formation of the Methodist societies gave a permanance to the gains achieved. Then there was the noble army of lay-preachers who extended and consolidated the movement by their heroic labours wherever there were people to whom they could preach.

Having been won to the Saviour, a new song must be raised from the hearts of the people. It was the poetic Charles who gave them the vocabulary and expression in his great hymns.

England entered the eighteenth century with a national sigh of despondency. Within the latter half of the century the gloom gave place to boundless song. A thousand tongues employed in proclaiming the great Redeemer's praise was a common sight and a pleasing sound.

Here was Wesley's greatest legacy to the nation - not a movement so much as a transformed England!

The succeeding pages are yet another account of the England John Wesley lived in as a young man. But it is more. It is a record of the England which Wesley left as his lasting memorial to a life of apostolic power and blessing.

This publication is sent forth with the express desire that others will prove God as Rev. John Wesley did in his day. May the Spirit who motivated the father of Methodism motivate the people of God in the closing years of this century. We too must catch the vision and experience the passion which sends us forth to snatch poor souls out of the fire and quench the brands in Jesus's blood.

E. STEWART

# 1
# THE CONDITION OF A NATION

The eighteenth century is one of the most remarkable periods in English history. Every century brings its changes but in one hundred years the country underwent an almost complete revolution. Dr. Luke Tyerman, the great Wesleyan historian stated, "Never has a century risen on Christian England so void of soul and faith as that which opened with Queen Anne, and which reached its misty noon beneath the second George - a dewless night succeeded by a sunless dawn. There was no freshness in the past and no promise in the future."

It was said by Professor Thorold Rogers in his work "Six Centuries of Work and Wages", that "no part in the Western world had evidenced so little change in fortunes, life, and habits as rural England between the reigns of Henry III and George III." A period of over five centuries.

Life proceeded with the monotony of a dull dead level, especially in rural areas. The countryside itself is indicative of the national spirit of that era.

Essex was forest land; Abingdon to Gloucester, a distance of some fifty miles was waste-land; Cambridge, Huntingdon, Derbyshire and Nottingham and all the way to the Scottish border was no different. The Eastern Counties were either fen-land or swamp-land.

To travel after night fall was fraught with danger. The few

who ventured across such desolate areas were guided either by directional light houses or ringing bells. Thus they may be spared the great danger of losing their way entirely. Wildlife found a great haven in such a wilderness. Wild boar, wolves, foxes, red deer, wild bulls, wild cat, marten and badger roamed freely. Eagles, buzzard and crane flew over the Eastern marshlands.

In Traill's "Social England", we read "there were still twenty-two million acres of waste and unenclosed land in 1795 according to an agricultural survey". The country was, in the main, wooded waste, swamps and great expanses of barren landscape.

Let us bear in mind this was after tremendous strides of advance during the latter half of the century.

What shall we say of the road network? It was practically non-existent! Arthur Young states that "ruts four-foot deep and floating mud comprised eighteen miles of thoroughfare between Preston and Wigan - during a wet summer"! Can one conceive the condition of the roadway during Winter? Essex roads were so narrow it was said 'a mouse could scarcely pass a carriage'.

Wesley, the experienced horseman, would often slip the reins of his faithful horse allowing the animal to pick its steps between ruts, potholes, and obstacles. In such times animal instinct was more keen than human endeavour. The landscape was but an articulation of the spirit of the nation. The century was born in desolation but in the Providence of God the same century experienced a mighty generation. A great silent revolution in agriculture, industry and religion breathed life into the valley of dry bones.

The rural life of the nation was significantly influenced by the genius of Viscount Townshend, nicknamed Turnip Townshend (1674-1738), the father of mixed farming and rotational cropping procedure.

Jethro Tull (1674-1740) gave the working man the implements to till the land by inventing the horse-hoe and the seed drill machine.

Robert Bakewell who died in 1795 at Loughborough pioneered in-breeding of horses, sheep and cattle. He was the stock-breeder par excellence.

It will be obvious at a glance that the combined fruit of these men's labours provided feeding for the stock and food for the nation, as well as taming the wilderness.

On the industrial front a similar story unfolds. The industrial dominance of Britain was secured by the inventions of the art of smelting iron by means of coal; the steam engine of Watt, the spinning jennies and mules of Hargreaves, Arkwright and Crompton; the foundation of the woollen industry in the West Riding through genius of the Doncastrian parson Cartwright; Wedgwood's discovery of porcelain manufacture, and the improvement of transit by the canals of Brindley, and the roads of Telford and Blind Jack of Knaresborough.

What underlying influence effected this remarkable turnabout in the English nation? The answer lies in the great evangelical awakening of the century!

It was a movement which infused divine life into the barren wasteland of human hearts. Any history of English life in the eighteenth century which by-passes the Wesleyan revival, is incomplete. It fails to locate the nerve centre of England's glorious hour.

Whatever changes we find in the field or factory, there is none so striking, so far-reaching, so stirring as the transformation of the people of the nation. England needed God in an acute sense. The spiritual desolation was of all the most unparalleled. It was this challenge which called for a response. Could the prevailing tide be turned? What was the prevailing mood which John Wesley inherited as an Englishman born in 1703?

## ENGLAND'S SOCIAL STATE

The population of England experienced no appreciable increase between the fourteenth and seventeenth centuries. During the eighteenth century there was an estimated increase from five and a half million to over eight millions. We get some idea of the condition of the country when we take a glance at the larger centres of population.

Wesley's London had a mere six hundred thousand people, Liverpool thirty-four thousand, Leeds seventeen thousand, Manchester and Salford twenty-seven thousand. Yorkshire was an impoverished county with a sprinkling of little towns dotted over its dales. In the earlier part of the century the country was comprised of small towns and villages. These were surrounded by wasteland, forest, or swampland.

On the western side Bristol had thirty-three thousand inhabitants. Yet this was the second largest centre of population in the entire country.

In consequence of the geographical desolation there was little inter-communication between centres of population. In 1770 Arthur Young said "there were but four roads in England; the rest would be a prostitution of language to call turn-pikes".

Turnpike roads were established principally during the second half of the century by 'turn-pike trusts' which were really private enterprises which established a toll system for the general upkeep of roads as well as the formation of new mileage. Despite these efforts the road system was made up of steep gradients, deep runnels, projecting rocks, morasses, quagmires, by courtesy called roads.

Before 1750 it took four days by express coach to travel from London to Liverpool. The mail coach took ten days in Summer and twelve more in Winter for the same journey. From Norwich to London took two days in Summer and three in Winter. The Flying Coach from Manchester to London required four and a half days! This was an incredible speed according to its advertisers. But by 1780 those speeds had been doubled between Liverpool and the metropolis and quadrupled on the Manchester line. The zenith of speed was recorded in 1798 by one traveller who had covered ninety miles in seventeen hours.

A quick mathematical calculation makes it a speed of just

over five miles per hour.

In addition, the roads were generally cluttered with pack-horses, teams of oxen, donkeys and even dog-teams, not to mention bogged down carriages and slow moving gentry. From these conditions the words 'slow-coach' and 'post-haste' were coined and are still freely used to this day. In addition to all these inconveniences the highwayman was never far away. He was the menace of the age for the travelling public.

All these conditions put great restriction upon any extended measure of travel. It explains why Wesley's arrival in town or village was such an occasion of amazement.

A strange face in the town was the whole topic of conversation with the inhabitants.

Regardless of this great social restriction, Wesley encompassed the country. Birrell says, "Wesley paid more turnpike tolls than any man who ever bestrode a beast!"

Class distinction prevailed in the eighteenth century. On the bottom rung of society there were the working-class people. They were the colliers, agricultural labourers, porcelain workers, and weavers. Agricultural wages per week ranged between 5s. 2d. in Gloucester and Wiltshire, and 1s. 4d. in Kent and Middlesex. Weavers earnings averaged 8s. 7d. per week. Colliers took home 11s. 0d. per week at Wakefield and 15s. 0d. a week at Newcastle. Cutlery workers earned 13s. 6d. at Sheffield.

The scenes of deprivation and poverty at this level of society were quite appalling. Little children wrought for a mere pittance. Wheaten bread was beyond buying. People lived from hand to mouth. In old age they lived off the parish or went to the workhouse. One in every five of the working class population was reduced to dire extremity.

Little wonder infant mortality was so high, and many children died before reaching the age of ten. Parents bore large families but the deprivation fostered disease on every hand. A staggering seventy per cent of young children who were boarded out from overcrowded workhouses died each year as a result of neglect.

Boys and girls, as well as women, worked in slave-like conditions. Little boys four or five years of age were hired for four pounds to crawl through the chimney flues. Five pence a day was paid to the children for eighteen to twenty hours work in the mines. These and many other enormities are recorded by J.H. Whiteley.

Next on the scale of ascent there were the shopkeepers and traders. Life was not easy for the local shopkeepers. Transportation of goods was slow. In consequence supplies were usually limited. Market day brought some life to the town but generally the day was whiled away in the sunshine or gossiping at the ale-house.

Life for the commercial class was relatively pleasant, especially when placed alongside the working class. Fifty thousand Huguenot refugees, with their varied skills, sparked off a period of industrial progress. Trade in linen, paper, hats, tapestry, glass, pottery, clothes and calicoes mushroomed in the kingdom. Export of these wares greatly increased the cash turnover in the country and for the traders themselves.

The most grievous burden was taxation. The cost of maintaining the army and navy, royal allowances and governmental departments must be met. National debt stood at fifty two millions in 1714 with an interest bill of three million three hundred thousand. As a result everything was taxed: salt, currants, malt, coal, glass, silk, soap, candles, leather, paper, linen, calicoes, land, property, and windows. Public outcry went unheeded. The taxation of imports resulted in a gigantic smuggling trade along the coast which in turn necessitated an army of revenue officers patrolling the coastline in an effort to apprehend the offenders. The Upper Class lived within the ring fence of good Society. A casual glance will show us this was far from good in the Scriptural sense. They were an extravagant, wine-drinking, often immoral, and foul-mouthed category. Lower classes were disdained. Politics, literature and art employed their conversations as they whiled away their time in the taverns of the day.

Walpole, the long-serving prime minister, was a master of political corruption. Judges swore on the bench. The king swore incessantly at the top of his voice. A lawyer's clerk said of a certain lady who called for an appointment without leaving her name, "I could not make out who she was, but she swore so dreadfully, she must have been a lady of quality". It was none other than the Duchess of Marlborough.

Such was the general image presented to society by these people. Thankfully there were some who were pious and generous in both the middle and upper class.

## CRUEL JUSTICE

The criminal code was severe. Ferocious laws were placed on the Statute-Book and they were enforced. Poverty and misery produced crime which was in turn carried out with criminal viciousness.

Sydney in his book "England and the English" says:- "To steal a horse or sheep; to snatch property from the hands of a man and run away with it; to steal to the amount of forty shillings from a dwelling house or privately to the value of five shillings in a shop; to pick a pocket of only twelve pence and a farthing; these offences all continued until the end of the eighteenth century to be punishable with death."

There were one hundred and sixty offences listed on the Statute Book as punishable by death and this was augmented by many more as the century unfolded.

Public execution at Tyburn was a common event. Ten to twelve offenders were executed at a time! Some forty to fifty could be condemned at a single court-sitting.

These were regular events for petty offences.

Other horrendous barbarities were inflicted on criminals. Burning at the stake for women guilty of murdering their husbands, public flogging and crushing to death, were some of the methods employed.

Indeed the public excitement rose to fever pitch as the death carts made their way from prison to scaffold. Ringside seats could be bought from six pence to two shillings.

It is most appropriate to make passing reference here to that noble Methodist soul-winner, Silas Told. He exercised an outstanding ministry to prisoners. He accompanied the malefactors to the gallows exhorting them to trust Christ. Wesley said at his funeral, "The greatest part of those whom Silas attended died in peace and many of them in triumph of faith."

Prisons were foul-holds of disease, squalor, and over-crowded by the wretches of society. Bedding was but filthy straw; food was nauseous and scanty; prisoners were heavily chained; vicious intercourse, sickness, and neglect prevailed.

Simons records that "in 1749 the noxious fumes from Newgate prison attacked and eventually claimed the lives of two judges, the Lord Mayor, one alderman, and about sixty other persons while conducting courtroom proceedings in the Old Bailey Sessions House".

In spite of gallant attempts by General Oglethorpe and John Howard to effect some measure of prison reform, their appeals fell on deaf ears.

The ruling class of people were not interested. Thanks be to God for the consistent labours of Wesley and Whitefield as they sought to present the gospel of hope for the soul in these dreadful dungeons.

Such was the picture of social England. A land of isolated towns and villages. Local dialects and intermarrying resulted as a consequence. Within towns there were the sub-divisions of class with little sympathy passing between. Wages were meagre, and work was painfully hard. Prisons were dreadful and criminal proceedings tended to dole out the ultimate penalty.

## ENGLAND'S MORAL CONDITION

While the general moral condition leaves much to be desired let us not forget that there were many people who practised Christian principles. Simon says:- "The praise of virtue led to its practice in innumerable English homes."

Even in the hour of moral depravation the Lord had His

people. They were the lights in a crooked and perverse society. God has always had His witness, be it ever so feeble, against the great tide of iniquity which existed.

Let us look briefly however at the prevailing moral mood and practice of the country in the first half of the century at least.

## THE THEATRE

Here was the chief form of amusement for Society, and it was generally coarse, obscene and scandalous.

Addison confessed in 1712 "that it was one of the most unaccountable things in that age, that the lewdness of the theatre should be much complained of, so well exposed, and so little redressed".

Wesley declared "the stage is the sink of all profaneness and debauchery."

Addison said "As matters stand at present multitudes are shut out from theatre by reason of those abuses and corruptions that accompany it. A father is often afraid that his daughter should be ruined by those entertainments . . . The accomplished gentlemen upon the English stage is the person that is familiar with other men's wives and indifferent to his own, as the fine woman is generally a composition of sprightliness and falsehood. "

In 1719 a certain chaplain in a nobleman's house denouncing the horrid blasphemies and impietes of the English Theatres, demonstrated that the plays of the day offended against no fewer than fourteen hundred texts of the Bible.

Sir John Barnard raised the issue in parliament in 1735 complaining that the London Theatres were corrupting youth, encouraging vice and debauchery and generally prejudicing trade.

John Wesley passed the same 'scathing' judgement on theatres in his letter to the Mayor of Bristol in 1764.

"Theatrical performances sap the foundation of all religion . . . are peculiarly hurtful to a trading city . . . giving a wrong turning to youth. Attendant evils are drinking and debauchery producing indolence, effeminacy and idleness . . ."

It was William Law who wrote on the absolute unlawfulness of the Stage saying it is "as certainly a house of the devil as the Church is the House of God."

## CRUEL SPORTS

Something of national mentality and morality is seen in the prevailing sports. Football, cricket, bowls, golf, tennis and other games formed the better side of English sport. Unfortunately there was the darker element.

Cock fighting, cock-throwing (played by tying the legs of the bird together and throwing it on sharp spikes), bull-baiting, bull racing, falconry, badger baiting, pugilism and cudgel play were the popular blood sports of the day. Phenomenal sums of money were placed on the prestigious cock-fights through the land. Sometimes one thousand guineas were at stake. The cruelty attached to these events is quite distressing reading.

## LOTTERIES AND GAMBLING

The gambling of the sports arena proceeded to the ale-houses and gambling houses which were licensed for all manner of dice games. Government approved lotteries were rife all over the land. Between 1709 and 1724 the Government raised immense sums of money by lotteries. Whiteley says "the aristocracy accepted a tradition of imperturbable recklessness in all forms of gambling."

Travelyan described society as "one vast casino; wherever half a dozen met, whether for music or dancing, for politics or drinking the waters, the box was sure to be rattled, and the cards out and shuffled".

## DRUNKENNESS

Leckey the historian says 1724 was the year "when gin-drinking began to spread with the rapidity and the violence of an epidemic. The fatal passion for drink was at once, and irrevocably, planted in the nation".

The soaring consumption of liquor is evident in the following figures. These are the quantities distilled in the various years.

| | |
|---|---|
| In 1684 | 527,000 gallons |
| In 1714 | 2,000,000 gallons |
| In 1727 | 3,601,000 gallons |
| In 1735 | 5,394,000 gallons |
| In 1742 | 7,000,000 gallons |
| In 1750-51 | 11,000,000 gallons |

A common bill-board hung out by the gin-retailers announced that their customers could be made drunk for a penny, dead-drunk for two pence with free straw provided in the cellars for bedding.

Mark Pattison said in his essay on Tendencies of Religious Thought in England 1668-1750:-

"The historian of moral and religious progress is under the necessity of depicting the period as one of decay of religion, licentiousness of morals, public corruption, profaneness of language - a day of rebuke and blasphemy".

"It was an age destitute of death or earnestness, an age whose poetry was without romance, whose philosophy was without insight, and whose public men were without character; an age of light without love whose very merits were of the earth, earthy."

## ENGLAND'S RELIGIOUS STATE

Mr. Fitchett makes the comment that "every century is blackened by human wickedness in greater or lesser measure". The truest judgement of any nation or period is the tone of its religion - or what passes for religion. What was the quality of the ministry of the day?

Again it must be said there were divines who laboured faithfully to please their Master in Heaven. Over against the few there was the great majority who indulged themselves in loyalties and abandonments which stripped the church of fidelity and national influence.

A number of factors paralysed the church's witness. The Deistic controversy made its inroad, and produced its scepticism. The tragedy was, the church had no power of resistance. While some divines won battles on the intellectual level it would have taken spiritual fire to establish a resounding and permanent victory. The church did not possess such, even in its more orthodox precincts.

Political subservience wrought havoc and brought cringing disgrace to religion. The monarch was the head of the Church. Those who know the record of the monarchs can understand the attitudes of the bishops. Under Queen Anne, at the commencement of the century, and the succeeding monarchs, we have a picture of pitiful servility. Bishops curried favour with the sovereign, hoping for promotion. Simon says "ecclesiastical fortunes were in the monarch's hands. Ambitious men were consumed with a passion for preferment and their only hope of gaining high office lay in standing well with the court".

The avarice for power and money is well documented by Mr. Whiteley. "Men gained high office not because of hard work and piety, but through string pulling, and coat trailing exercises. Such men conveniently winked the eye at immorality in high places. Their consciences were far from being void of offence. In addition they became proud and insensitive to all beneath them".

As for the men of inferior rank in the ministry, the same fatal defects of character existed. All enthusiasm was banned from the pulpit.

The first great duty of religion was to be tepid. There must be no enthusiasm, no heroics. Whether zeal or moderation be the point we aim at, let us keep fire out of one and frost out of the other.

Leslie Stephen said of one of the most famous preachers of the times namely Hugh L. Blair of Edinburgh:-

"He was a mere washed-out dealer of second-hand common places, who gives the impression that the real man has vanished and left nothing but a wig and a gown".

Dr. Skevington Wood records the assessment of Oliver Goldsmith on the clergy:-

"Their discourses from the pulpit are generally dry, methodical, and unaffecting, delivered with the most insipid calmness, insomuch that should the peaceful preacher lift his head over the cushion, he might discover his audience, instead of being awakened to remorse, actually sleeping over mechanical and laboured composition".

In addition to these dilutions of religion many of the younger clergy were profane. They had no scruples regarding their associations and pursuits. Dr. Stoughton reproduced the following testimony of a cleryman at that time. "The public have long remarked with indignation that some of the distinguished coxcombs, drunkards, debauchees, and gamesters who figure at the watering places, and all places of public resort, are young men of the sacerdotal order."

The combined effect of these events was a church void of the supernatural in its doctrines, stripped of its authority and besmirched in its ethical virtue in the eyes of the public.

In addition to all these elements the Church was in no-man's land.

Puritanism had spent its energy. The Non-conformists had been engrossed in politicing, and subsequently, intrigue and secularization blunted the keen edge of this early Presbyterianism. In course of time the cancer of Arianism, with its denial of the deity of the Lord Jesus Christ, ate the vitals of the movement. Unitarianism became the doctrinal executioner and Skeats says in his "History of the Free churhes":-

"In less than half a century the doctrine of the great founders of Presbyterianism could scarcely be heard from any Presbyterian pulpit in England. The denomination vanished as suddenly as it had arisen; and excepting in literature, has left little visible trace of the greatness of its power".

Thus we find that whether we look at the State Church or the dissenters, there was an abysmal lack of true spiritual power. Not even the earlier influence and memory of a Bunyan,

Doddridge, Watts, or Richard Baxter could retrieve the blessing.

In fact the very enthusiasm and passion which was evidenced at the birth of Puritanism must never again be entertained within religion. It upended the status quo and therefore must be avoided. 'Please do not disturb', was the fitting epitaph over religion. Enthusiasm precipitates change and that is not desirable.

It was indeed, "A dewless night succeeded by a sunless dawn."

There was no freshness in the past, and no promise in the future. The Puritans were buried, the Methodists were not born. The world had the idle, discontented look of the morning after some mad holiday, and, like the rocket-sticks and the singed paper from last night's squibs, the spent jokes of Charles and Rochester lay all about, and people yawned to look at them. The reign of buffoonery was past, but the reign of faith and earnestness had not commenced.

# 2

# THE MAKING OF A MAN

On the north-western edge of Lincolnshire lies the isle of Axholme. It was so called, being a small strip of land, neither marsh nor fen, which was bounded by five waterways. The Idille and Torne flowed on the west side; the Trent on the east; the Dorne on the north; and the Bykers-Dyke on the South. The principal town on this ten mile by four strip of reclaimed land was Epworth. This was the settlement of about two thousand inhabitants. Apart from market day it was a quiet habitation over which there stood the commanding tower of the local old church.

The old rectory had just been restored after an accidental fire during the early part of 1703. It was now a commodious timber and plaster building with a thatched roof. On the ground floor were seven main rooms, a kitchen, a hall, a parlour and a buttery. Besides the attics there were three large bedrooms upstairs. The barn, a great timber structure was thatched with straw, and in the dovecote the rector's family played their childhood games.

The children's joy increased with the news that a new baby brother had arrived - a brother for thirteen year old Samuel; twelve year old Emilia, eight year old Susanna, seven year old Mehetabel, and Anne who was just one year old.

It was the 17th June 1703. The fifteenth of nineteen children born to Samuel and Susanna Wesley, he was called John Benjamin in memory of two previous brothers who had died in infancy. The observant reader will note that sorrow and loss were not uncommon to the rector and his beloved wife. Yet in the providence of God, all their losses were going to be more than compensated for in the person of John. What a prodigy he would be in the history of England, and the world! Because of the striking nature of his pedigree we must make some enquiry regarding it at this point:-

## THE FAMILY TREE

It was not until after his remarkable conversion that John Wesley paid much attention to the quality of his forebearers. But writing to his brother Charles in 1768 he said:-

"Such a thing has scarce been heard a thousand years before, as a son, father, grandfather, atavus, tritavus, preaching the Gospel, nay, and the genuine Gospel in a line".

Wesley came in a straight line of clerical heritage. His sacerdotal descent can be taken a generation further to his great grandfather, Bartholomew Wesley. He was a son of Sir Herbert Westley of Westleigh, Devonshire and Elizabeth De Wellesley of Dangan, County Meath in Ireland. A student at Oxford, he studied medicine and divinity. He was not to know that his son John; grandson Samuel and three grandsons would follow in his footsteps.

Bartholomew was a man of strong convictions. He married the daughter of Sir Henry Colley of County Kildare in 1619. He became rector of Catherston, Dorset in 1640. It was in September 1651 that the flight of Charles the Second to France was almost jeopardised but for the long prayers of Mr. Westley. Charles and his retinue spent the night at the village, being unable to make their boat connection. The local blacksmith, seeing their horses had been shod in the North of England, became suspicious of the visitors, and decided to alert the minister. Mr. Westley was reading prayers and could not be disturbed. By the time he was available Charles had made good his escape. Said Westley, "If Charles ever returned he would be sure to love long prayers because he would surely have snapt him had prayers been over earlier."

In 1662 Bartholomew was ejected from his charge under the Act of Uniformity. Indeed his son John was imprisoned in 1661, for not using the Book of Common Prayer. He was also turned out of his living in 1662. He had been a devout and promising student earning the special notice of the great puritan divine, Dr. John Owen, then vice chancellor of Oxford. A cameo of his life is given by Professor Schmidt as being one who possessed:-

"The proud consciousness of having been sent, which yet unreservedly subjects personal activity to the judgement of the Bible, the determination to conform to primitive Christianity, the stress on visible results as the fruit and conversion as a definite aim."

Because of the iniquitous laws of the time, he was harried from place to place. A spirited non-conformist like his father, he preached for the famous Joseph Alliene and other non-conformists of his day. He was an excellent soul-winner, a man of the common people and an executor of good deeds. He was imprisoned on four occasions and died in 1671, a relatively young man at the age of thirty four. His equally fine and fiery father passed away shortly afterwards, and was buried at Lyme Regis beside the sea.

Mr. Telford says the "John Wesley of the eighteenth century was a true successor to this great and good grandfather".

His itinerant ministry, his care for the fisher-folk, his unflinching loyalty to his principles, his success in winning souls, and his simple godly life were all reproduced in his illustrious grandson. The first John Wesley was cautious, moderate, and singularly open to conviction.

He was survived by his widow for thirty-two years, as well as a large family one of which he called Samuel, later to become Rector of Epworth.

Though born of non-conformist blood Samuel turned his back on non-conformity and with no resources other than those supplied by his precocious talents and marvellous literary activity, he maintained himself at Oxford, where he prepared for the ministry of the Established Church.

Fitchett says "the family assistance he received accumulated to five shillings but he graduated with a degree and ten pounds fifteen shillings in his pocket".

On the whole no student perhaps ever gave less to Oxford or got more out of it than Samuel Wesley. One cannot help feeling amused at the historic captions placed upon him. He was a loyal little man, loved his children, was clever and hard working but he could never keep out of debt.

Of his major work, a commentary on the book of Job, it might have been esteemed as a new exercise in patience to that much afflicted patriarch, had be been required to read it. Bishop Warburton said "Poor Job! it was his eternal fate to be persecuted by his friends."

Whatever his limitations, he was either clear-sighted or providentially guided in his marriage to Miss Susanna Annesley. Like her husband-to-be, she had analysed the Dissenting school and turned from it and her father's theology. Dr. Annesley was a dignified and liberal-minded non-conformist divine. Daniel Defoe who married one of his daughters said in tribute to his preaching:-

"The sacred bøw he so divinely drew
That every shaft both hit and overthrew".

The epitomy of godliness, he passed away in 1696 with these precious exclamations, "I will die praising Thee . . . I shall be satisfied when I awake with Thy likeness - satisfied! satisfied!" Such manliness, godliness and serenity coupled with methodicity, rubbed off on his very accomplished daughter. He had instilled the most noble principles into the maiden who would in process of time give the world its John and Charles Wesley who in turn inherited this legacy of high resolve.

Susanna was the twenty fourth child of the Annesley family. During her thirteenth year 1682 she met young Samuel Wesley at her sister's marriage to John Dunton the famous bookseller.

Maybe the common decision of these two young people to leave the dissenters that year helped to kindle the love flame which eventually brought them together in 1688.

It is not unusual that the union produced the remarkable off-spring which we now revere.

Concentrated in the leading figure of the eighteenth century awakening, we have an ancestry of will power spanning at least three previous generations. Fitzgerald says, "They were men the world could not bend and found it next to impossible to break".

There was the influence of Puritanism at its best with its educational standards, disciplined devotional and moral teaching and intense theological discussion times.

Also there was the love of conformity and respect for established authority found in Anglicanism. All these and more virtues met under the roof of the Epworth rectory. Out of the mill of heredity came a man, a personality, a new and original force, which impressed its own stamp on the eighteenth century, and altered the currents of history for all time. Puritan, preacher, poet, - each of his ancestors contributed some potent element of character, but the John Wesley whom we have to study was more than the sum of them, and different from all of them, a man with great individuality - a "man sent from God".

## THE EARLY YEARS

Susanna Wesley was an Anglican by denominational allegiance but a thorough-going Methodist by practice. Life at the rectory ran like clockwork. The same principles, if applied today by the nation's motherhood, would lead to happier homes and a better society.

An extended leter from Mrs. Wesley to her son John in 1732 gives account of the family rules.

"The first three months of life were mostly spent in sleep with dressing, undressing and feeding carried out at fixed times. After this they were laid in their cradles awake, and rocked to sleep. Sleeping time was gradually reduced from the maximum of three hours each morning and afternoon until no daytime sleep was required. Around one year old they were taught to respect the chastening rod and to cry softly. The result was a generally quiet household. Meal times were thrice daily with no eating between times. As soon as possible they sat at the meal table, acquired ability to use any tableware and asked for things politely. At six, after the family observed family prayers they had supper; at seven the nurse maid washed them and by eight all were in bed and left to go to sleep without supervision".

The key to success lay in conquering the child's will at the outset of life. This subjection proceeded at a constant temper until there was implicit obedience. The heart of the matter lies in these words spoken by Susanna Wesley:-

"I insist upon conquering the will of children betimes because this is the only strong and national foundation of a religious education; without which both precept and example will be ineffectual. But when this is thoroughly done, then a child is capable of being governed by the reason and piety of its parents, till its own understanding comes to maturity, and the principles of religion have taken root in the mind."

## EPWORTH ACADEMY

Mrs Wesley instructed her children both religiously and educationally. She was the school mistress and the catechiser of Epworth parsonage. Respect for devotions was emphasised from the beginning of life. Morning and evening prayer started with the Lord's Prayer. As time proceeded other collects, catechism and scripture readings were added. Language was always chaste, promises were not broken, another's property must never be taken. If there was a misdemeanour, confession averted punishment.

Day school commenced at five years of age. The first day from nine to twelve and two to five the alphabet was learned. Then followed spelling, reading, first a line, then a verse (Genesis ch.1 v.1.).

No lesson was left until it was perfect.

What a beautiful contrast existed in the rector's house when we look outside. People's habits were filthy and appetites were bestial. Children were treated brutally, most were illiterate and the offspring of the rich were spoilt.

Walter de la Mare, commenting on the Wesley code said, "Is it conceivable that any child thus brought up could come to a bad end?"

The memory of the devastating fire which reduced the rectory to ashes was etched on Wesley's mind for life. He recalled it forty years later and offered praise to God for his miraculous deliverance.

## FIRE AND FURY

"At eleven o'clock it came to my mind that this was the very day and hour in which forty years ago I was taken out of the flames. I stopped and gave a short account of that wonderful providence. The voice of praise and thanksgiving went on high and great was our rejoicing before the Lord."

Henry Parker's work of art has compassed land and sea capturing in vivid detail the raging inferno fanned by the strong easterly wind.

The livestock are being hurried from their stables; the Wesleys, bereft of clothing, and clad in scanty night attire, huddle together. The central drama depicts a group of men with a resourceful figure astride their shoulders. Strong arms reaching up, take hold of the little boy as he releases himself from the bedroom window. The boy was six year old John Wesley. It was the 9th February 1709. Almost simultaneously with his escape the entire roof came crashing into the house. The man is unknown but he preserved a priceless gift for the world that night.

As the courageous man carried the little bundle of life to the rector he cried out "Come neighbours, let us kneel down; let us give thanks to God! He has given me all my eight children; let the house go; I am rich enough."

John Wesley referred in later life to himself "as a brand plucked out of the fire". When he sat for his portrait before George Vertue, the backdrop was a house in flames and the words beneath read, "Is not this a brand plucked out of the fire?" - words taken from Zechariah ch.3.v.2.

Indeed in 1753 when he was exceedingly ill that he despaired of life, he penned the wording for his headstone, "Here lieth the body of John Wesley, a brand plucked from the burning."

It becomes clear that the drama and deliverance of that night was eventually spiritualised in the personal experience of Wesley for it was his brother Charles who said on 24th May 1738 "a brand, not only once, plucked from the fire."

Wesley's great vocation in life was viewed as a rescue mission to consuming humanity. They must be rescued as poor souls out of the fire and as brands quenched in Jesus' blood. It may be enquired, How came the fire in the first place?

It was believed by John and his father that the whole event was malicious.

Without going into detail, four issues are worthy of mention.

There was bitter rivalry between the Dissenters and the High Church party of the Church of England. Samuel created many enemies in his support of the latter party and his stand against the former.

Secondly, this support was transmitted into his political affiliation with Toryism and voting for High-Church candidates.

In the third instance, he acted rashly at times with a dishonest set of parishoners, who were only too happy to support their fellow thief, and vent their malice against someone who exposed them.

Fourthly, they were naturally vicious, zealous and uninhibited when it came to expressing their feelings. They were little better than Christian savages, and it was no unusual thing for them to vent their hatred by burning the crops and the farmsteads of those whom they regarded as their enemies.

Thankfully their evil design failed to effect the ultimate

catastrophe - the incineration of the Wesley family as they slept in their beds.

Settling back after a few months, in their new rectory, Mrs. Wesley declared "I do intend to be more particularly careful of the soul of this child, that Thou hast so mercifully provided for, than ever I have been, that I may do my endeavour to instil into his mind the principles of Thy true religion and virtue. Lord give me grace to do it sincerely and prudently, and bless my attempts with good success".

Could any maternal resolution have paid greater dividends in modern history? Certainly not!

## NEW HORIZONS

It was January 1714 when news came from the Duke of Buckingham that John had received a nomination to further schooling at Charterhouse.

He was leaving the shelter of home for the big city of London. He entered the historic mansion house as a boarder when scarcely eleven years of age. He was one of forty four boys in his group, all gown-boys, the traditional uniform of the school but not, it must be hastily added, reared in rectory style.

Life was very different now. He was taught by Headmaster Walker. The big boys were bullies. They organised raids on the meat supplies of the juniors. One was fortunate to have bread, and Wesley seemed to sustain himself almost exclusively on such fare.

Six years were spent at Charterhouse before gaining admittance to Christ Church, Oxford. He was on his way to the great university. He entered with a scholarship worth forty pounds per annum and a recommendation from Charterhouse masters as "a very promising classic with a special gift for Latin verse".

For five years the undergraduate applied himself with diligence to his studies. This was not the general state of young men at Oxford. Time was whiled away, and degrees were handed out almost solely for residence. Finances were always on the bottom line. The spectre of poverty hovered above

Wesley.

His health was less than full. Thinking a haircut would improve his health, mother encouraged a visit to the barber. His reply was that "unless his health became quite poor he would not part with a precious two or three pounds per year in such a manner."

Wesley was a diligent, successful student. He took his Bachelor 's degree in 1724. In 1725 he was made Fellow of Lincoln, and a year later he was appointed lecturer in Greek and Moderator of the Classics. He took his Masters degree in 1727, no mean academic feat in a total of seven years.

Wesley's total sojourn at Oxford falls into three categories of time and character.

Between 1720-1724 he was the vivacious student. During the next three years he was the sombre mystic. The quest for God intensified considerably. He aquired Thomas a Kempis's book "The Imitation of Christ" and Jeremy Taylor's "Holy Living and Holy Dying", and William Law's "Serious Call". He entered for the Christian ministry and was ordained a deacon on September 19th, 1725.

This event appears to have motivated John to an earnestness hitherto unknown. He began to set apart an hour or two every day for religious meditation. He guarded diligently against all sin in word or deed. He set his heart towards inward holiness. The spiritual quest was now in earnest. He followed a rigorous timetable in addition to his college commitments.

He read widely amongst manuals of discipline, the writings of the Church Fathers (of which "Macarius the Egyptian" sharpened his desire for perfection) and the devotional books already referred to.

During this year 1725, Wesley was particularly challenged by Jeremy Taylor's "Holy Living and Holy Dying". He corresponded with his mother regarding its content. He was an agonising soul, endeavouring to satisfy the Law but only too aware of an inward antagonistic law warring in his members and hindering the highest desires of his soul.

This persisted during his Oxford days. In 1727 duty called.

Samuel, the father, required assistance at Wroot. John took leave of the university until 1729. He returned to the spires and corridors of Oxford in 1729 where he remained until 1735.

Now he was the energetic Methodist.

Thirty two years had passed since his infant eyes saw the light of day. Each decade of life had been a concentrated pursuit of life's ideals. From a human perspective the man had been made.

Culture, decorum, diligence, academic achievement, excelling in logic, and still possessed of a godly fear. All these were distilled in the life of John Wesley.

But providence had more in store for both man and nation!

# 3

# THE BIRTH OF A MOVEMENT

The developing period of any large-scale movement in the history of the church is marked by various and seemingly incidental events. Men who have made history did not always set out with that intended purpose. They stepped into the breach when the occasion demanded it, and found upon reflection, they had etched their names in granite. Great doors often swing on small hinges. Great matters are kindled by small fires. A multiplicity of minor events coupled together under divine providence produce startling results. Nowhere is this maxim more applicable than in the rise of the movement called Methodism.

When the apostle Paul wrote to the people at Corinth he said, "All things are yours; whether Paul, or Apollos, or Cephas, or the world, or life, or death, or things present, or things to come; all are yours; and ye are Christ's; and Christ is God's."

In other words, nothing is lost in the eternal Christ. All the circumstances of life are parts of His way, links in the chain, cogs in the wheel; all are vital and effective in bringing to fruition His eternal design. Let us consider some of the contributing factors which gave us the Methodist movement.

## THE RELIGIOUS SOCIETIES

The general description of the condition of England outlined in the opening chapter is beyond dispute. It was a social, moral and spiritual wilderness. A spiritual paralysis prevailed. Yet when we take a closer look at the situation we see harbingers of blessing. The murmur of the divine breeze can be detected half a century earlier than in the great awakening. Altering the simile it may be said that here we have the 'small cloud, the size of a man's hand.' It was the precedent of the abundance of rain which drenched the land during the mid-eighteenth century.

The Religious Societies are inextricably linked to the Methodist awakening. Some knowledge of the background and nature of their operations is essential to our understanding of Methodism.


## THEIR INCEPTION

During the reign of Charles II, a German preacher, Dr. Andrew Horneck expounded the Word of God at Savoy. The awakening sermons drew large audiences. Another soul of like spirit delivered morning lectures at St, Michael's, Cornhill resulting in deep conviction of sin in many of the hearers.

A number of young men, seeking to lead a holy life, began to meet once a week with the purpose of applying themselves to good discourse and to things wherein they might edify one another.

The most distinctive account of the original Societies, which sprang from this soul-concern in the laity of the church, comes from the pen of Dr. Josiah Woodward. His book entitled, "Account of the Rise and Progress of Religious Societies in the City of London" went through four editions by the year 1712.

Describing the condition of some of the young men in London and Westminster he said:-

"They were touched with a very affecting sense of their sins, and began to apply themselves in a very serious manner, to religious thoughts and purposes".

"The common concern of each drew them together".

They needed little other language but that of their looks to discover their inward sorrows to each other; they needed no other arguments to incline them to pity each other's case, but to consider their own, there being a propensity in nature to succour those who groan under the like miseries with ourselves. So that by these and the like means, they soon contracted a very intimate acquaintance.

"They were devout members of the Church of England, and in their desire to progress Godward they consulted with and sought advice from their minister who decided that since their troubles arose from the same spiritual cause, and that their inclinations and resolutions centred in the same purpose of a holy life, they should meet together once a week and apply themselves to good discourse and things wherein they might edify one another. And for the better regulation of their meetings, several rules and orders were prescribed them, being such as seemed most proper to effect the end proposed. Upon this they met together, and kept to their rules, and at every meeting they considered the wants of the poor, which in process of time, amounted to such considerable sums, that thereby many poor families were relieved, some poor people set into a way of trade suitable to their capacities, sundry prisoners set at liberty, some poor scholars furthered in their subsistence at the university, several orphans maintained, with many other good works".

It was in the year 1680 that a volume, "The Country Parson's Advice to his Parishoners" was first published. The subject material of the book set forth guidelines for the operation of the Societies. It had no author's name, but was republished in 1701. This was the book which greatly influenced John Wesley around 1730. It was distributed and studied by the members of the Holy Club, to which we shall refer later.

## THEIR RULES

Dr. Horneck became the adviser to a number of the Societies formed by him. He drew up a list of rules for the regulation of the meetings.

All that enter the Society shall resolve upon a holy and serious life.

No person shall be admitted into the Society until he has arrived at the age of sixteen, and has been first confirmed by the bishop, and solemnly taken upon himself his baptismal vow.

They shall choose a minister of the Church of England to direct them.

They shall not be allowed, in their meetings, to discourse of any controverted point of doctrine.

Neither shall they discourse of the government of the Church or State.

In their meetings they shall use no prayers but those of the Church, such as the Litany and Collects, and other prescribed prayers; but still they shall not use any that peculiarly belongs to the minister as the Absolution.

The minister whom they choose shall direct what practical divinity shall be read at these meetings.

They may have liberty, after prayer and reading, to sing a psalm.

After all is done, if there be time left, they may discourse with each other about their spiritual concerns; but this shall not be a standing exercise which any shall be obliged to attend unto.

One day in the week shall be appointed for this meeting, for such as cannot come to the Lord's Day; and he that absents himself without cause shall pay threepence to the box.

Every time they meet, everyone shall give sixpence to the box.

On a certain day in the year, viz. Whit Tuesday, two stewards shall be chosen and a moderate dinner provided, and a sermon preached, and the money distributed (necessary charges deducted) to the poor.

A book shall be bought, in which these orders shall be written.

None shall be admitted into this Society without the consent of the minister who presides over it; and no apprentice shall be capable of being chosen.

If in any case conscience shall arise, it shall be brought before the minister.

If any member think fit to leave the Society, he shall pay five shillings to the stock.

The major part of the Society shall conclude the rest.

The following rules are more especially recommended to the members of this Society, viz. to love one another. When reviled, not to revile again. To speak evil of no man. To wrong no man. To pray, if possible, seven times a day. To keep close to the Church of England. To transact all things peaceably and gently. To be helpful to each other. To use themselves to holy thoughts in their coming in and going out. To examine themselves every night. To give everyone their due. To obey superiors, both spiritual and temporal".

With these guidelines the original Societies came into existence. Under Dr. Woodward these rules were expanded and adopted into the Religious Societies of his day. It is obvious that the chief element was holiness of heart and life. The primary rule of the Popular Society of which Dr. Woodward was minister or overseer, reads thus:- "That the sole design of this society being to promote real holiness of heart and life, it is absolutely necessary that the persons who enter into it do seriously resolve, by the grace of God, to apply themselves to all means proper to accomplish these blessed ends".

It ought to be said that between the time of Dr. Horneck and Dr. Woodward, there had been a partial collapse of the Societies under the reign of James II. With the accession of William and Mary the trend was reversed and Dr. Woodward's rules were widely adopted.

There were some forty such Societies at the time of Dr. Woodward's writing. They were to be found in London, Oxford and Cambridge as well as other cities and towns.

## THEIR DECLINE

It appears that with the passing of years the original vigour left the Societies. A number of factors contributed to their decline. They seem to have become involved in certain political issues of the day. The fact that they were under the exclusive direction of the clergy was detrimental to their spiritual life. Second generation clergy were not of the same spiritual calibre as their predecessors. They produced a deadening influence upon the members. The people also confused the Societies with another movement called the Society for the Reformation of Manners, a movement which had occasioned much hostile criticism and consequently people avoided the Societies.

It was going to require more than ritualism to change the country. The best characteristics and the finest rules must have the breath of life from above. Yet they continued to exist. They became part of society and their principles were well founded. The Holy Spirit was not utterly finished with them as a vehicle which He could employ for the glory of God. We shall return to the Society meeting in due course.

## STREAKS OF DAWN IN WALES

The greatest effect of Wesley's work was felt in England but we must trace the movings of the Spirit elsewhere. There is a sovereign purpose in the heart of the Eternal which is not confined to national boundaries. When He begins to initiate a divine movement in one area, it is not uncommon for it to break forth in other areas also.

Rev. John Tennant witnessed a gracious movement of the Spirit in 1730-1732 in the Presbyterian church at Freehold, New Jersey. In 1734 Jonathan Edwards saw a similar outpouring in Northampton, New England. But the Lord had blessing in store for the British Isles also. He condescended to work in the principality of Wales. As is usual, the Lord took up some frail human vessels, filled them with His divine power and sent them forth. Their labours were strikingly effective.

## GRIFFITH JONES

In the parish of Llanddowror, Carmarthenshire, in South Wales, Griffith Jones preached the gospel with remarkable success. Little is known of his conversion but it was followed by great blessing. In 1713 at Langharne he began preaching beyond the bounds of his own parish. The crowds ranged between five hundred and a thousand people at each service. Sometimes it was reckoned there were three to four thousand hearers, many of them non-conformists. He obviously had a powerful appeal right across the religious spectrum.

He preached with great feeling often with tears running down his cheeks.

William Williams, another earnest soul-winner and hymn-writer for the Methodists said of Jones:-

"Here's a man who broke forth a little before the break of dawn, a bright glorious star shining amid the night's threatening clouds, a man whose clear trumpet call was heard by many".

His other outstanding contribution to revival was the establishment of the "Circulating Schools". Between 1737-1761 some three thousand two hundred and twenty five schools were founded in sixteen hundred different locations.

Almost half the Welsh population of four hundred thousand people, from six to seventy years of age learned to read the Bible in the Welsh language. Thus was the seed-bed laid for the soon coming itinerant evangelists.

Griffith Jones later withdrew his public support from the Methodists, but it is felt that his heart sympathy continued to lie with them despite differences of opinion. He has been called the "Morning Star of the Methodist Revival." It is a justifiable epithet to a great preacher and educator who by his preaching and schools, gave the Methodists a Daniel Rowland, Howell Davies and Howell Harris, and whose schools became virtually synonymous with Methodist Societies. But we must allow the focus of attention to proceeed.

## DANIEL ROWLANDS

In his evangelistic travels Griffith Jones was expounding the gospel in the village of Llanddewi, Brefi, which lay about five miles from its neighbouring village of Llangeitho, Cardiganshire. His keen eye picked out a sceptical looking young curate in the congregation. A brief heart cry went up to the throne of grace for the young man's conversion, and subsequent usefulness in soul-winning.

Mr. Jones did not know that he was looking at an intellectually brilliant and tremendously fit young athlete. He was curate to his brother John in Llangeitho after having been ordained in 1734 in London, a journey which he had undertaken on foot. Eighteen months had passed since that March journey. Sunday afternoons were spent on the sports field, enjoying the thrills and popularity of the occasion.

With gentle compassion Mr. Jones observed him for a moment, pointed at him and said, "Oh for a word to reach your heart young man!!"

The succeeding year is quite interesting.

An independent preacher called Phillip Pugh, who was also a Dissenting Minister in the neighbourhood, was drawing large congregations. He was a "thundering" preacher. Rowlands felt that therein was the secret of his power. Consequently he became serious, studious and also a thundering preacher. He preached the terrors of the Law, the pangs of the lost, and the holiness of God. People flocked to hear him. Church graveyards, as well as the buildings, were filled. Men and women were physically prostrated on the ground, under conviction of sin.

John S. Simon records that "at least an estimated one hundred members of Rowland's congregation were under deep conviction before the preacher himself began to seek the Lord".

After two years of law-preaching, Pugh said to Daniel Rowlands:-

"Preach the Gospel to the people, dear Sir, and apply the

balm of Gilead, the blood of Christ, to their spiritual wounds, and show the nesessity of faith in the crucified Saviour". "I am afraid" said Rowland, "that I have not that faith myself in its vigour and full exercise".

"Preach on it" said Pugh, "till you feel it in that way; no doubt it will come. If you go on preaching the Law in this manner, you will kill half the people in the country, for you thunder out the curses of the Law and preach in such a terrific manner, that no-one can stand before you".

The result was both powerful and widespread. Instead of groans of despair, there were shouts of praise and victory. The church at Llangeitho experienced some wonderful events.

One Sunday morning, Daniel Rowlands was preaching. He became so enthused in the ministry of the Word and the people became so engrossed in the message, that the hours slipped by unnoticed. It was only when the sun rays streamed through the Western door of the church that preacher and congregation were aware that it was now sunset. Whereupon the people were quickly dismissed.

Edward Morgan records a very striking incident in Mr. Rowland's ministry. "During the reading of the Litany for the Lord's Day service a powerful visitation of power and feeling gripped Rowlands. Coming to these words his whole frame was seized with passion. By thine agony and bloody sweat, by Thy cross and passion, by Thy precious death and burial, by Thy glorious resurrection and ascension, and by the coming of the Holy Ghost."

"The congregation seemed electrified, falling down in a large mass together, there being no pews in the church. Evidently the time to favour the land, God's set time, was coming".

Yet again we must reluctantly leave this great servant of God for another area in the Welsh principality. There is yet another conspicious dawn-light of the awakening.

# HOWELL HARRIS

He was born at Trevecca in the parish of Talgarth, County of Brecon on January 23rd, 1714. He followed the ways of the world until on March 30th 1735 at a communion service he heard the minister say, "If you are not fit to come to the Lord's Table, you are not fit to come to church, you are not fit to live, nor fit to die".

The Spirit of God began to reveal sin and produce deep conviction in Harris's soul. On Whit Sunday May 25th 1735, he was again at Communion. He had come across the sentence, "If we would go to the sacrament simply believing in the Lord Jesus Christ, we should receive forgiveness of all our sins".

"In the solemn moment of participation at the table he recalls:- "I was convinced by the Holy Ghost that Christ died for me, and that all my sins were laid upon Him. I was now acquitted at the bar of justice, and in my conscience. This evidenced itself to be the true faith, by the peace, joy, watchfulness, hatred to sin, and fear of offending God that followed it".

It was a new world to Howell. His soul was filled with an insatiable desire for the salvation of sinners. He testified to some on his way home from Talgarth. They simply stared at him, and well they might, he felt, since he himself had never heard anyone confess to assurance of salvation. Yet he was assured and remained convinced.

It had been a unique immediate encounter between a trusting soul and a saving God. Likewise Harris seems to have passed through a personal Pentecost on June 18th 1735. He was kneeling in prayer alone when suddenly his heart was filled with the fire of divine love. He could only cry out "Abba Father, Abba Father".

"I knew that I was His child, and that He loved me and heard me. My soul being filled and satisfied cried, "It is enough; I am satisfied. Give me strength and I will follow Thee through fire and water! I could say I was happy indeed! There was in me a well of water springing up to everlasting life; and the love of God was shed abroad in my heart by the Holy Ghost."

During that summer Harris was deeply distressed by the godless nature of the people. After Sunday service the people were taken with a universal deluge of swearing, lying, revelling and gaming, which swept through the country like a torrent.

No reproof came from the pulpits. Harris went to prayer with a few people of kindred spirit.

Afterward he went forth, and conversed with the needy neighbours, then he spoke to some who had been awakened. Eventually, he held forth the truth with burning conviction and zeal.

It was during November that Howell Harris made his way to Oxford. Unfortunately for Harris he arrived too late to meet John and Charles Wesley. The little band, of which we shall speak later, had disappeared. The Wesleys had gone to Georgia on missionary work. It was a lonely life for the Welsh man. He yearned for his people and their salvation. He decided to return to the hills and valleys of Wales.

In 1736 he founded a school at Trevecca and also several Religious Societies like those mentioned earlier. Griffith Jones was also associated with this project.

It is of interest to note that as a result of Harris's increasing itinerant preaching, with such blessed results, Religious Societies were being formed. They were not related to the now formalised Societies of Dr. Woodward, except that the seed-thought may have come to Harris through Woodward's writings. Mr. Hughes makes the point that "the earliest societies may be regarded as the first-fruits of Welsh Methodism, and all Methodism".

Alongside a successful ministry we have mob violence and legal opposition as well as clerical antagonism. But Howell Harris was not faint-hearted. He blazed a trail for God, and in spite of this great mischief levelled against him, said that he "was carried on the wings of an eagle triumphantly above all".

Howell Harris's work was successful. He preached to immense crowds, founded many Religious Societies, and drove back the flood of godlessness that threatened to overwhelm the country. His name still shines with special radiance in the annals of the religious life of Wales.

In addition to these Welsh worthies Simon makes a brief reference to Howell Davies. His work was executed with remarkable effect. The Pembrokeshire countryside in particular experienced a spirit of revival in which many were won to the Lord. Communion services were thronged with waiting communicants.

The combined effects of these four men changed the moral and spiritual scene in Wales. The characteristics of their work are but a miniature demonstration of that great awakening which was soon to follow.

## HUNGERINGS FOR GOD AT OXFORD

We must now turn to England in an effort to detect the first awakenings in the kingdom. We must of necessity travel back in time before we detect the various preparatory elements which Providence employed.

## FOCUS ON CHARLES

A full picture does not emerge unless we turn our attention to John's younger brother Charles. He entered Oxford in 1726. He was sprightly and active, apt to learn but not given to the same religious seriousness as John. Life at Oxford was a great and happy event. There were new friends to meet, and new avenues for his enthusiastic personality. Pressed, as he was at times, by serious John he replied, "What! would you have me to be a saint all at once?"

One biographer says "He was orderly in nothing but his handwriting, which was exquisite."

He had no vice and much attractive virtue. He loved and respected his brother John, but he was more of a harum-scarum.

The period of crisis in his life came after John's departure to Wroot. He had to take a personal stand for a religious mode or drift down-stream with the general crowd. The providential movings of God brought him to diligence which led to serious thinking.

How this change came about remains shrouded in mystery. We can only make conjecture from his own correspondence with John in January 1729, the year following this remarkable change of direction.

"God has thought fit, it may be to increase my wariness, to deny me at present your company and assistance. It is through Him strengthening me, I trust to maintain my ground till we meet; and I hope that neither before nor after that time I shall relapse to my former state of insensibility. It is through your means, I firmly believe, that God will establish what he has begun in me; and there is no one person I would so unwillingly have to be the instrument of good to me as you. It is owing, in great measure, to somebody's prayers, my mother's most likely, that I am come to think as I do; for I cannot tell myself how or when I awoke out of my lethargy - only it was not long after you went away".

He began to attend the sacrament of the Lord's Supper weekly. His daily life was formulated around religious issues. He was preparing for holy orders with an earnestness of soul before unknown.

Coincidental with his new devotion, was a deep concern among the tutors regarding the lowering standard of morals and general ungodliness at Oxford. Deism had produced its debilitating effects among the students.

The Vice-Chancellor, supported by his tutorial staff, sent out instruction that there must be a more diligent pursuit of sound principles, and orthodoxy. Students should, by Canon Law, have been in attendance at Communion at least once each week.

Instead, the whole rule was neglected, and indeed to do such a thing, only called forth remark and ridicule.

Charles, with his natural charm, drew a little group of fellow-students around him. They were also in pursuit of God. They began to meet regularly; they undertook to support each other; duties were taken seriously and executed with precision. They went to Christ Church for the Sacrament week by week. It wasn't long until the sceptics and scoffers began to stigmatise them, The Godly Club, Biblemoths, and Sacramentarians. But is was the ordered fashion of their lives that finally settled the name. They were called Methodists. Given in derision, the title stuck and has since become the denominational name.

The original band of Methodists was made up of Robert Kirkham, William Morgan, James Harvey, George Whitefield, and Charles Kinchin, not forgetting Charles Wesley who formulated the club in the first instance.

## THE RETURN OF JOHN

On October 21 1729 Dr. Morley, the rector of Lincoln College sent a letter to John Wesley. It was a strong request for him to return and reside in his capacity as Junior Fellow and class moderator. Wesley complied and duly arrived from the parish at Wroot on November 22 1729.

On his arrival he found the group in existence. He joined it and due to his natural endowments, zeal, influence, and keen intellect he soon became its leader.

The momentum quickened. The fellowship met every evening to lay plans for the next day. During early 1730 the prisons were being visited, the sick were being comforted, help was being given to the poor, and children were being educated.

They attracted the admiration of some and the ridicule of many. Robert Kirkham informed them that he had been much rallied the previous day for being a member of 'The Holy Club'.

Here we have yet another nickname which has become firmly settled in the history of Methodism.

Despite some failing fortunes in their number by 1731, they experienced a revival in 1732.

John Clayton a Manchester Grammar School boy joined them through the witness of John Wesley. It was also during the course of this year that a key member William Morgan passed away. Being hard pressed by opposing elements, the little band of Methodists were given fresh life and status through the support of the influential William Law.

But with the best will in the world, Wesley had to face realities. The little Society was coming to an end. He was now in greater demand in wider fields. Samuel senior was coming to the end of the journey. There were preaching engagements and in addition, former members were taking up life vocations in different fields. The one singular event which transpired at its later period was the transformation of George Whitefield.

He was introduced to the Methodist movement through his breakfast meeting with Charles. He became one of the strictest members of the Holy Club. He abstained from good food, fasted twice a week, lay prostrate on the ground in agonising prayer for his soul, and dressed like a pauper.

After about seven weeks, he was enabled to lay hold on Christ by a living faith, was filled with peace and joy, and became probably by far, the most happy member of the Oxford brotherhood.

As for the others they sought salvation by the deeds of the Law. Wesley wavered between concepts of salvation by faith, as expressed through some of his sermons and pamphlets, and salvation by works, as manifest in his practical living.

Oxford Methodism was not perfect by any stretch of the imagination. It was a dark, austere, misty quest for God. Tyerman says "but for the ministry of the Wesleys, Whitefield and a few others its memory might, without public loss, have been buried in oblivion".

Six years of mechanical prayers, pious services, physical austerities, were like a spiritual treadmill. Was Wesley being steered toward the goal by an unseen hand? Were the unrealised joys attainable by some other means? What more could be done to procure the seemingly unobtainable?

## WESLEY TURNED MISSIONARY

April 25 1735 John and Charles watched their father pass from this scene of time. His closing utterances were precious and peculiarly prophetic, "Be steady! The Christian Faith will surely revive in this kingdom. You shall see it, though I shall not". To John he said, "The inward witness son - the inward witness! that is the strongest proof of Christianity."

He died, happy in the Lord, though as always, a debtor. They laid him to rest, and the landlord seized the livestock to cover the unpaid rent on the land. The sons departed with the old man's literary masterpiece, a Commentary on the Book of Job. It was to be presented to the Queen. In London the brothers met a certain Dr. Burton. He was one of the trustees of a newly founded colony in America named Georgia.

After their introduction to General Oglethorpe the founder of the colony, the proposition of missionary service was put before Wesley.

A clergyman was required to preach to the new settlers as well as the native Indians. John Wesley was the prime choice. Educated, zealous, a capacity for work, a churchman; just what he needed! Would he venture? If his mother, for whom he was now responsible, agreed, it might be a possibility.

Unexpectedly, for his part, she supported the proposition without reservation. Others advocated the same course of action. Subsequently the neat little churchman, schooled to the letter, religious to the fingertips, boarded the ship "Simmonds" on October 14, 1735.

It was an experiment spanning two and a half years. Before embarking he writes on October 10, 1735. "My chief motive is the hope of saving my own soul."

On October 14, he records in his journal:- "Our end in leaving our native country was not to avoid want . . . nor to gain the dung or dross of riches or honour; but singly this - to save our souls; to live wholly to the glory of God".

The reader can read between the lines, the progress and success of the venture by another entry in the journal dated January 24, 1738:- "My mind was now full of thought; part of which I wrote down as follows:- "I went to America to convert the Indians: but oh! who shall convert me? Who, what is he that shall deliver me from this evil heart of unbelief?

"It is now two years and almost four months since I left my native country, in order to teach the Georgian Indians the nature of Christianity: But what have I learned myself in the meantime? Why (what I least of all suspected) that I who went to America to convert others, was never myself converted to God".

Was the entire exploit profitless? Would it have been better if he had never gone? The venture precipitated some profound blessings and some awful embarrassments. The blessings remain, the embarrassments are better forgotten. God can bring good out of evil and He did for Wesley.

The brothers found twenty six German travellers on board for the outward voyage. They turned out to be Moravian missionaries. During the voyage violent storms erupted. It seemed as if all might be lost. Mr. Wesley, who had been since his embarkation, the zealous organiser of religious devotions, prayers, and preaching was now a trembling soul. His companions were, on the other hand, engaged in song!!

"Were you not afraid"? asked Wesley. "I thank God, no", "But were not your women and children afraid?" "No our women and children are not afraid to die".

Wesley had been face to face with death. The prospect haunted him. He was not equipped for such an eventuality.

Indeed he drew a parallel between the rough and the smooth sea. The former is a life torn up by the storms of human passion, and the latter a mind calmed by divine love.

"Clearly he had himself in view", says Dr. Skevington Wood.

The next extremely personal interview came shortly after landing on American soil, February 6, 1736.

On the following day, Oglethorpe, who had proceeded a short journey up the Savannah river, returned with Spangenberg. He was the spiritual leader of the Moravian settlement, and second in command to Count Zinzendorf the famous Moravian leader. What a pungent, personal encounter that proved to be! The men took to each other. They conversed and then Wesley enquired about his vocation, and sought advice regarding how to conduct himself in this new environment. Spangenberg replied:- "My brother, I must first ask you one or two questions. Have you the witness within yourself? Does the spirit of God bear witness with your spirit that you are a child of God?" "I was surprised and I knew not what to answer". He observed it, and asked, "Do you know

Jesus Christ?" I paused, and said, "I know he is the Saviour of the World". "True", replied he, "but do you know He has saved you?" I answered, "I hoped He has died to save me". He only added, "Do you know yourself?" I said, "I do", But I fear they were vain words".

The succeeding months were marked by disillusionment. the people were with few exceptions, gluttons, drunkards, thieves, dissemblers, liars. They were implacable, unmerciful murderers of fathers, murderers of mothers, murderers of their own children.

Wesley ran into deep trouble by applying his rigid ecclesiasticism at every point. He even refused the Lord's Supper to the godly pastor Johann Bolzius on the ground that he was not an episcopally ordained priest.

Eventually, he was faced with legal proceedings because he had refused to give communion to Sophey Williamson on the grounds that she had been neglectful of the means of grace. Some felt it was spitefulness on Wesley's part, since he had, sometime previously, an unhappy love affair with her. Be that as it may, Wesley stuck by his ritualistic guns, was exonerated by the court, but lost the good-will of the people. He was forced, through all these happenings, to pack his belongings and sail back to England. It was the month of December 1737. He had been preceded by Charles fifteen months earlier.

The venture was not fruitless if we recall the two great discoveries he made by it; namely that there was an experience of God which removed the fear of death, and even more so that he had never been converted to God himself.

He must yet pursue a personal salvation, and he was more aware of this than ever.

His homeward voyage was lonely, heavy hearted, and self-abasing. Wesley had time to brood. Why had this theology, devotion and self-sacrifice proved such an utter failure under testing?

The missionary who was sailing from America was very different in spirit to the missionary who had sailed to America. Mysticism was not the answer, ritualism had failed, ascetic austerities proved fruitless.

Wesley was being prepared for another teacher, and a new experience. He landed at Deal on February 1, 1738, conducted morning prayers and preached at his lodging house. He then proceeded to London, to give account of his work in Georgia before the colony trustees. He met Charles who was surprised to learn of his return. On Tuesday 7 February he renewed acquaintance with the Moravian community and with one Peter Bohler, the man who would profoundly influence his life.

It was a day much to be remembered.

## THE WONDERFUL BIRTHDAY

The succeeding four months were the most momentous in the Wesleys' lives. On the evening of February 3 John arrived in London. He renewed acquaintance with Rev. John Hutton and his son James who now owned a book shop 'The Bible and Sun' near Drury Lane. Here he met Charles, anxious to hear a first-hand account regarding Georgia. Previous to John and Charles' departure for Georgia John had preached with great effect on 'The one thing needful - the renovation of fallen man'. James Hutton reformed and a Religious Society in his father's house had been quickened. After branching out into his own business he established a Religious Society at Islington and another in his home. This well organised Society progressed until outgrowing its accommodation, it was continued in the church at No 32 Fetter Lane.

James Hutton was to figure in the divine plan for Wesley.

Leslie Church enumerates five significant dates which mark Wesley's spiritual progress.

Firstly, **February 7,** the day already alluded to when Wesley went to the house of a Dutch merchant, Mr. Weinantz. Here he met Peter Bohler. Bohler and two companions had just arrived from Germany en route for Georgia in America. Peter who had joined the Moravians as a lad, had been educated at Jena University. He was ordained by Count Zinzendorf and when Wesley made his acquaintance was just twenty six years of age.

It was this charming young man whom God employed to guide the two Wesleys to the blessed assurance of salvation.

Wesley, learning that they had neither acquaintance nor lodging in London, procured a place for them near Mr. John Hutton's house at Westminster, where he himself was staying at that time.

This threw the two men closer together and they conversed deeply on spiritual issues.

Bohler described the brothers John and Charles very graphically. John was "a man of good principles, who knew he did not properly believe on the Saviour, and was willing to be taught."

"Charles was persistently very much distressed in his mind, but not knowing how to begin to be acquainted with the Saviour."

On **February 17** John and Charles travelled to Oxford with Peter. The weekend was spent in long conversations regarding spiritual things.

There were opposite views. Bohler spoke of faith; Wesley reasoned; they perplexed each other. Wesley records in his Journal March 18, 1738:- "All this time I conversed much with Peter Bohler, but I understand him not"; and least of all when he said "My brother, that philosophy of yours must be purged away".

After a few days John took leave of Charles and Peter, travelled back to London, preached at a few services and visited his mother. Suddenly an S.O.S. altered all his plans - possibly his future career. Charles was critically ill with pleurisy - and possibly dying.

Back to Oxford he hurried, and providentially, to Peter Bohler. Two days later he arrived. Charles was improving and Peter was joyously speaking to him of saving faith.

Sunday **March 5** was another critical date for John. Of this date he writes in his Journal account:- "I was on Sunday the 5th, clearly convinced of unbelief of the want of that faith whereby alone we are saved. Immediately it struck my mind, "Leave off preaching. How can you preach to others who have not faith yourself?"

It was at this point Bohler's famous reply came to Wesley's query, "what can I preach?" He said. "Preach faith till you have it; and then because you have it you will preach faith".

The following day Wesley took the step and preached saving faith to a condemned prisoner. It was a remarkable transition at least in Wesley's mental conception of salvation. He had never preached salvation by faith alone, before this occasion. He had now crossed his Rubicon.

Telford notes a further crucial event on April 1st from the Journal. Wesley's heart was so full, after having pointed another prisoner to Christ on 27th March that when he went to Mr. Fox's society meeting at Oxford he broke free from ritualism.

"I could not confine myself to the forms of prayer which we were accustomed to use there. Neither do I propose to be confined to them any more; but to pray indifferently. With a form or without, as I may find suitable to particular occasions".

After preaching on the text, "The hour cometh, and now is, when the dead shall hear the voice of the Son of God, and they that hear shall live" he recorded April 2nd, "I see the promise but it is afar off"

He felt a crisis was drawing closer!

**April 22-23** marked a further definite advance. Wesley agreed with Bohler's definition of faith.

It was a sure trust and confidence which man has in God, that through the merits of Christ, his sins are forgiven, and he reconciled to the favour of God. He also agreed that happiness was the proper result of such faith.

Wesley could not support belief in an instantaneous work however. Back to his Bible again, he was astonished to find this was the biblical pattern! But then again, times have changed. It must be confined to apostolic times.

Bohler then produced the witnesses. Three or four men testified before Wesley and bore witness to the instant nature of regeneration. Wesley wrote tersely but competently, "Here endeth my disputing. I could now only cry out, Lord help Thou my unbelief!"

On May 1st three days before Bohler's departure for America, a little Society was formed at Fetter Lane as mentioned earlier. Charles, though averse to the new faith at that date was convinced by it on May 3. The next day the young Moravian had taken his departure. A very touching note is made by Wesley May 4.

"Oh what a work hath God begun, since his coming to England! Such as one as shall never come to an end, till heaven and earth pass away".

The succeeding days were marked by soul struggle. His preaching became more personal and vital. People were fascinated; the clergy were frightened; pulpits were systematically closed to him. He persevered in spite of it.

Let us trace the sacred dealings of the Spirit as the crisis approaches.

Charles was lodging with Mr. Bray, a brazier in Little Britain Street, near Aldersgate. On May 19 he lay ill, being still affected by the pleurisy attack.

A Moravian William Holland who was a painter visited him. He took Luther's Commentary on the Epistle to the Galatians. He left and Charles reflected on the closing verses of Chapter 2 "He loved me and gave Himself for me". If only he could realise that 'me' meant Charles Wesley. He laboured, waited and prayed to feel it. On Whit Sunday May 21st his prayer was answered! Hallelujah!

"I now found myself at peace with God, and rejoiced in hope of loving Christ . . . I saw that by faith I stood . . ."

On Tuesday May 23 Charles broke forth into new vigour, his physical strength returned, everything seemed new.

He must get up. He must write. He must sing - yes; that was it, he must sing. There was too much for one song - too much for six thousand though God was to spare him to write them. Pen! Paper! Ink!

Where shall my wondering soul begin?
How shall I all to heaven aspire?

A slave redeemed from death and sin.
A brand plucked from eternal fire.
How shall I equal triumphs raise,
Or sing my great Deliverer's praise?

John, more lonely than ever trudged on wondering, expecting. Charles was through. What about himself?

**May 24.** About five in the morning he opened his testament: "Whereby are given unto us exceeding great and precious promises that by these ye might be partakers of the divine nature" - 2 Peter 1.v.4. Just before going out he read again, "Thou art not far from the kingdom of God," Mark 12 v.34. The afternoon was spent at a service in St. Paul's. The anthem seemed appropriate.

Out of the deep I have called unto Thee
Oh Lord: Lord, hear my voice. O let Thine
ears consider well the voice of my complaint.
If Thou, Lord, wilt be extreme to mark what
is done amiss: Oh, Lord who may abide it?
For there is mercy with Thee; therefore
shalt Thou be feared. Oh Israel trust in
the Lord: for with the Lord there is mercy
and with Him is plenteous redemption.
And He shall redeem Israel from all his sins.

He left, deep in thought; the evening drew on. Here again we can only assume that it was James Hutton's little Society meeting gathered for worship. Among them was John Wesley. He writes the now immortal account:-

"In the evening I went very unwillingly to a Society in Aldersgate Street, where one was reading Luther's preface to the Epistle to the Romans. About a quarter before nine, while he was describing the change which God works in the heart through faith in Christ, I felt my heart strangely warmed. I felt I did trust in Christ, Christ alone for salvation: And an assurance was given me, that he had taken away **my** sins, even **mine,** and saved me from the law of sin and death".

The world must know, but first his brother Charles. He and

his friends dashed round to Mr. Bray's house, up the stairs and into Charles room.

"Towards ten, my brother was brought in triumph by a troop of our friends and declared 'I believe', We sang a hymn with great joy and parted with prayer."

The hymn was the one composed by Charles the previous day in memory of his own experience. They were singing a new song together.

It was a birthday - one of the great birthdays in the history of the world.

Leslie F. Church said:- "Here is a man transformed. In his troubled heart, deep peace at last. In his whole being strange new energy. Fifty years of amazing activity beginning. Fire running through stubble. The grace of God in England".

## EXPERIENCE HE LEFT

Three weeks after his Aldersgate Street exercise he set out for Germany. Wesley owed a great debt to the Moravian people through their courage on the "Simmonds", the searching interview with Spangenberg and the pilgrimage of faith with Peter Bohler. But he was hungry for truth. More light and instruction was vital.

At Marienborn he met and heard Count Zinzendorf preach on being justified and knowing it. The message reminded him of Peter Bohler's preaching. He proceeded on foot with his companion Benjamin Ingham to Herrnhut the Moravian settlement. He went, hoping to find living proof of the power of faith; people saved from inward and outward sin by the love of God shed abroad in the hearts, and from all doubt and fear by the abiding witness of the Holy Ghost given unto them.

He met them continually and, as he interrogated, watched and assessed these godly peasants, he was moved to write a revealing letter to Samuel his brother.

"I am with a Church whose conversation is in heaven, in whom is the mind that was in Christ, and who walk as He walked. Oh, how high and holy a thing Christianity is, and how widely distinct from that - I know not what - which is so called, though it neither purifies the heart nor renews the life".

He also noted other features of the community which became guidelines for his own work in later days. The constitution of the society, the school programme, the fellowship meetings, the conference at Marienborn, the love-feasts, etc. all helped to formulate a line of future action.

He would have gladly remained with Pastor Christian David and his friends, but the call of God was upon him. He bade his brothers and sisters farewell and started for England arriving back on September 16. The future plan was on the verge of being inaugurated.

"It would be difficult", says Matthew Lelievre, "to exaggerate the importance of this visit on Wesley's religious and ecclesiastical progress. The 'city of God' which he had beheld in Germany he was destined to reproduce in England, with such differences between a nation of an essentially reflective disposition, and a nation endowed with an active and enterprising spirit."

Methodism owes Moravianism special obligations. First it introduced Wesley into that regenerated spiritual life . . .

Secondly, Wesley derived from it some of his clearest conceptions of the theological ideas which he was to propogate . . .

Thirdly, Zinzendorf's communities were based upon Spener's plan of reforming the established Churches by forming 'little churches within them' in despair of maintaining spiritual life among them otherwise; Wesley thus organised Methodism within the Anglican Church.

Fourthly, in many details of his discipline we can trace the influence of Moravianism.

Once back on home soil he associated with the little Religious Societies in London, especially at Fetter Lane. The year was concluded with services in whatever pulpits remained open to him. But gradually he was being squeezed out into a new platform. He visited the prisoners at Newgate on a regular basis. Then in the providence of God, George Whitefield returned on November 30 after a ten month absence, having been in America raising funds for a proposed orphanage in England. He too was denied entrance to the church pulpits.

Thus at the inception of 1739 the principal members of the Oxford band of students were together in London. Each, in his own remarkable manner, had come into the joy of a living faith and all were poised to enter a new field of service.

Along with Ingham, Hall and Kinchin they had a "pentecostal season indeed" according to Whitefield.

Five days later they met for fasting and prayer and parted with a full conviction that God was about to do great things among them.

They had the message; all they required was the method. This was soon to follow. Whitefield set out for Bristol arriving on February 14 after an insurrection against his preaching at St. Margaret's, Oxford, on February 4.

He was given a bad press and found his name already blackened when he reached the western city. What should he do? Confine his temperamant, convictions, talents and message to a few Religious Societies and prisons? He surveyed the scene on February 15 and two days later he launched forth.

To him belongs the honour of preaching in the open air; something which was to be the outstanding feature of the Great Awakening. His congregation? The unchurched, ungodly and unsought miners and their families at Kingswood. Two hundred came to hear the first message of the new preacher in the open air. The movement had experienced its birthday.

# 4

# THE GROWTH OF THE WORK

The year of 1739 has been called 'the great Methodist year'. It saw the beginnings of Methodism.

The love-feast, an integral part of Moravianism, was incorporated into Wesley's structures. The first Methodist love-feast was held on January 1 1739 at Fetter Lane in London. Class meetings were formed, evangelistic field-preaching commenced, and the first Methodist Chapel was built in Bristol. It was a momentous year: one that gave the direction and guidelines to the whole after development of the Methodist movement.

Let us trace this remarkable year when the river of divine blessing began to flow in spate again.

## INITIAL GLEAMS OF GRACE

Already a brief account of George Whitefield's break with tradition at Kingswood, Bristol, has been noted. Back in London, Wesley was in the first flush of harvesting among the people. A letter to George Whitefield dated February 26, 1739 reveals Wesley's new and exciting involvement in the soon coming revival.

"Our Lord's hand is not shortened among us. Yesterday I preached at St. Katherine's and at Islington, where the church was almost as hot as some of the Society rooms used to be. I think I was never so much strengthened before. The fields after service were white with people praising God. Almost 300 were present at Mr. Simm's, thence I went to Mrs. Bell's, then to Fetter Lane, and at nine to Mr. Bray's, where also we only wanted room. Today I expound at the Minories at four, at Mrs. West's at six, and to a large company of poor sinners in Gravel Lane (Bishopsgate) at eight; so I expound before I go to him, near St. James' Square, where one young woman has been lately filled with the Holy Ghost and overflows with joy and love. On Wednesday at six we have a noble company of women, not adorned with gold or costly apparel, but with a meek and quiet spirit and good works".

"At the Savoy on Thursday evening we have usually two or three hundred, most of them at least thoroughly awakened".

"Mr. Abbot's parlour is more than filled on Friday, as is Mr. Park's room twice over; where I have commonly had more power given me than any other place . . ."

It is obvious from this schedule of meetings that Wesley was now intensely involved in a new and spiritually aggressive evangelism. However, it was within the confines of various houses and meeting places.

Both Whitefield and Wesley were preaching now with the whole heart, the former in the open air, the latter within the precincts of homes and public gathering halls.

On March 23 Mr. Whitefield felt constrained to write requesting Wesley's presence and help at Bristol. The numbers were vast by comparison to anything previously witnessed. Kingswood was aflame with excitement; colliers were flocking to the various preaching places; the people began to pour out from the city. A report in the Gentleman's Magazine at this time said:- "Whitefield preached at Hanham Mount to five or six thousand persons, and in the evening, removed to the Common, about half a mile further, where three mounts and the plains around were crowded with so great a multitude of coaches, foot and horsemen, that they covered three acres, and were compiled at twenty thousand people".

He moved into Bristol and held services in a large bowling green during the last week of March. Crowds of five to seven thousand listened to the proclamation of the glorious gospel. But the time to return to America was drawing nigh.

The work must not be allowed to die for lack of a preacher. Who could he turn to? His interest focussed on John Wesley! But would Wesley's prejudice against ecclesiastical irregularities prove too resolute? Would the already promising stirrings at Fetter Lane and the surrounding area appear too influential to permit Wesley's departure? Two letters, one from Whitefield and the other from his travelling companion William Seward arrived with John Wesley,

"I am but a novice" wrote Whitefield, "you are acquainted with the great things of God. Come, I beseech you; come quickly."

In fact Whitefield had proceeded to advertise the arrival of Wesley for the following week in the local journal. "Wesley hesitated; Charles objected; and the Fetter Lane Society disputed; but at length the matter was decided by casting lots".

On March 29 he mounted his horse and rode out toward the city of Bristol. He arrived two days later, weaving his way among the stalls and traders, a tired horse and a reluctant rider! The prospect was not to Wesley's taste. He dismounted outside Mr. Greville's grocery shop. He was brother-in-law to George Whitefield, and it was here the now famous evangelist was lodging. Whitefield was not in the house. There in the semi-darkness John weighed the pros and cons of the opposition. He believed souls could only be reached through the church, yet here they were being reached in the fields!

Judgement must be suspended until he saw for himself, the next day, April 1, 1739.

The door opens. The radiant young orator comes in, Mrs. Greville following. They clasp hands, sing and pray together. They were opposites. Whitefield an enthusiastic twenty three years old, Wesley a calculating thirty six years old.

Impulse was confronting self-control. Whitefield's emotion and Wesley's logic were face to face.

Still, the hour passed quickly. Eight o'clock and Whitefield, accompanied by Wesley, went to the Weavers' Hall where Whitefield addressed about one thousand souls. They afterwards shared their feelings until about midnight. Of that evening Mr. Whitefield said, "I was much refreshed with the sight of my honoured friend, Mr. John Wesley, whom God's providence had sent to Bristol. "Lord, now lettest Thou Thy servant depart in peace."

## A NEW FIELD OF SERVICE

The new day dawns, big with possibilities. During that eventful day Wesley was to accompany his friend. He would see and hear for himself, down at the bowling green at the Pithay, close to Wine Street. The assembled crowd was a large and impressive spectacle; six or seven thousand! At noon, after passing the mining communities, continuing over the waste ground, past the slag-heaps, they arrive at Hanham Mount. A similar congregation had assembled. They progressed to Rose Green where an estimated thirty thousand stood in reverent expectancy. Whitefield announced his hymn, and then that dramatic delivery with such overwhelming effect! It moved the audience as the wind moves the forest leaves. God was doing a new thing. It was Whitefield's farewell to the open-air multitudes in West England. But his day was not yet over. The evening saw Whitefield at Baldwin Street Religious Society. The throng was such that admission to the doorway was only possible by ascending a ladder to the roof of an adjoining house and climbing across the tiling. Wesley had gone to address a little company at Nicholas Street Religious Society. The remarkable thing was his choice of subject, which on reading, struck him with a new light. It was the Sermon on the Mount. What better example of field preaching could one find in the Bible?

Before bidding his last farewell Whitefield announced that John Wesley would preach next day in the brickyard at the farther end of St. Phillip's plain.

"I would scarce reconcile myself first to this strange way of preaching in the fields, of which he (Whitefield) set me an example on Sunday; having been all my life (till very lately) so tenacious of every point relating to decency and order, that I should have thought the saving of souls almost a sin if it had not been done in a church".

By the arrival of Monday he records again, "At four in the afternoon, I submitted to be more vile, and proclaimed in the highways the glad tidings of salvation . . . to almost three thousand people. His text came from Luke ch.4.v.18-19, "The Spirit of the Lord is upon me, because He hath anointed me to preach the gospel to the poor . . .". Wesley had discovered the lost people of England at last.

Wesley's diary expresses something of the inner feelings as he prepared for that great day.

Monday 2 April, 1739. He had arisen at 7.00 am singing within. On Tuesday, after taking the irrevocable step, he arose at 5.45 am. singing while he dressed.

The warmed heart was finding a new avenue of expression. His mind was made up, and though it was to him a cross, he pursued it relentlessly for fifty years.

That day (one of the most important dates) he made up his mind that the whole world was to be his parish and that he would preach in those cathedrals whose floors were the cobble-stones of market-places or the slag heaps about a pit head, the deck of a ship or the rough ground in the corner of a field-cathedral whose boundaries were hedges or walls or the sea-shore, and whose roof was the blue dome of heaven, built and consecrated by God.

Whitefield was the pioneer, but Wesley donned the mantle and took the practice to the borders of the succeeding century. It gave him a mobility otherwise impossible. Congregations were of such magnitude, that no building could have accommodated them. It brought him where the need was and where the needy people were.

He remained in the Bristol area until June 11, 1739. Apart from brief visits to London later that month, as well as September and November, and a brief tour of Wales and

Exeter, Wesley laboured at Bristol until the end of the year.

During those months Dr. Tyerman estimates that Wesley delivered approximately five hundred addresses, discourses, or expositions. Of these only about eight were indoors.

This city, therefore, occupies a unique position in Methodist history. He made it his chief centre over fifty years. Its people were his people.

## A PATTERN EMERGES

The focus of attention now settles on John Wesley. His friend George Whitefield had departed on his preparatory period before setting sail for America later that year.

Methodism ran to a plan from its inception.

In fact, it was the routine of the men, which provoked the title in the first place. On May 13, we have "the precursor of the multitude of Methodist 'plans' since issued".

Wesley's weekly plan emerged quickly:-

"My ordinary employment in public, was now as follows:- Every morning I read prayers and preached at Newgate. Every evening I expounded a portion of Scripture at one or more of the Societies. On Monday in the afternoon, I preached abroad, near Bristol; on Tuesday at Bath, and Two-Mile Hill alternately; On Wednesday at Baptist Mills; every other Thursday, near Pensford; every other Friday in another part of Kingswood; on Saturday in the afternoon, and Sunday morning, in the Bowling Green; on Sunday at Eleven, near Hanham Mount, at two at Clifton; and at five at Rose-Green! And hitherto, as my days so hath my strength been".

Telford states that his congregations at seven in the morning often consisted of five or six thousand people.

When he joined Whitefield briefly at Blackheath London on 14th June 1739, he addressed a crowd of twelve or fourteen thousand people.

This style of preaching, always a cross to Wesley, was nevertheless fundamentally dear to him. "It is field preaching which does the execution still; for usefulness there is none comparable to it", October 10, 1756.

Indoor preaching was akin to being cooped up and he urged his preachers to make full use of the open air .

"Preach abroad at Newry, Newtown, Lisburn, and Carrick, if ever you would do good. It is the cooping yourselves up in rooms that has damped the work of God, which never was and never will be carried out to any purpose without going out into the highways and hedges and compelling poor sinners to come in."

The reader will note that his exhortation came some twenty seven years after Wesley took that eventful step himself in Bristol city.

Necessity was the mother of invention, for it was in consequence of the closure of the church pulpits that these men turned to the only alternative remaining. By denying them the right to preach indoors, the clerics precipitated a ministry that might not have otherwise developed. From the divine perspective we know that "all things work together for good to them that love God" - Romans ch.8.v.28.

The Holy Spirit will not be straightened by the resistance of such instruments when the time for a visitation from on high approaches.


## A MESSAGE EXPOUNDED

The chief, almost only, aim was to explain to the people the plan of scriptural salvation. Wesley chose his preaching texts carefully. They had an immediate bearing on the great issue of personal salvation, through faith in the sacrifice of the cross.

Writing in 1748 in his famous "Plain Account of the People Called Methodists," Wesley says:- "The points we chiefly insisted upon were four. First, that orthodoxy or right opinions, is at best, but a very slender part of religion, if it can be allowed to be any part of it all; that neither does religion consist of negatives, in the bare harmlessness of any kind; nor merely in externals, nor doing good, or using the means of grace, in works of piety (so called) or works of charity; that is nothing short of, or different from the mind that was in Christ .

"Secondly, that the only way under heaven to receive this religion is, to "repent and believe the gospel;" or as the Apostle words it, "repentance towards God and faith in our Lord Jesus Christ.

"Thirdly, that by this faith, "he that worketh not, but believeth on him that justifieth the ungodly, is justified freely by His grace, through the redemption which is in Jesus Christ. And lastly that being justified by faith, we taste of the heaven to which we are going; we are holy and happy; we tread down sin and fear, and sit in heavenly places in Christ Jesus".

The exposition of such clear biblical truths, supported by the power of the Holy Spirit, made a profound impact upon the hearers.

In the Society rooms, God began to arrest members with divine conviction.

On April 17, at Baldwin Street Society, four persons cried aloud with utmost vehemence as if they were gripped in the agonies of death. Likewise at Weavers Hall, a few days later, and in greater measure again at Baldwin Street on May 1. The preaching of the Word of God touched people in the prisons as much as in homes.

## NEW STRUCTURES FOR FELLOWSHIP

These were exciting days! In fact before Whitefield took his departure from Bristol, he had suggested Wesley should write out orders for the 'Bands'. This he did on April 4 and that day the first little band, consisting of three women, was founded.

Their purpose was to meet together weekly, in order to confess their faults one to another, and pray for each other. That evening four young men agreed to follow suit. The two groups met separately. On April 17 eleven single women met and desired to include three others. They were sub-divided into the three bands. Wesley hoped to stimulate the life of other Society members who were cold and formal in their worship.

Here we have the roots of that great Methodist accommodation called the class-meeting. Fellowship is so vital to experience and the class-meeting was the outcome of that basic human quality; the desire for fellowship with kindred minds.

Fitzgerald terms this as "the most interesting event of the year."

Wesley challenged any would-be critics in a stern manner "How dare any man deny this to be (as to the substance of it) a means of grace ordained by God?"

God in His gracious superintending providence, crystallised into a network of little cells, those who were coming to the Lord.

In Wesley's "Appeal to Men of Reason and Religion," which was written in 1748, we have an account regarding the spontanaeous manner in which the class meeting and the Society were conceived.

## THE SOCIETY

The Society came about as a result of the people's desire to have Mr. Wesley address them on spiritual issues. He requested them to forward their names and addresses. The response was too great to treat each case individually. Wesley replied "If you will all of you come together every Thursday, in the evening, I will give you the best advice I can".

They, in course of time, named this a Society and it was inaugurated in London.

## THE CLASS MEETING

The Class Meeting which became so much part of Methodism took form in Bristol.

There were followers over a widespread area. Wesley was finding it increasingly difficult to watch their behaviour. As always, some tares grew among the wheat. Their behaviour was causing harm to the work. Let us follow Mr. Wesley's record of the events which transpired.

"At length, while we were thinking of quite another thing, we struck upon a method for which we have cause to bless God ever since. I was talking with several of the Society of Bristol concerning the means of paying the debts there, when one stood up and said, "Let every member of the Society give a penny a week till all are paid". Another answered, "But many of them are poor and cannot afford to do it", "Then", said he "put eleven of the poorest with me; and if they can give anything, well: I will call on them weekly; receive what they give and make up what is wanting". It was done. In a while some of these informed me, they found such and such an one did not live as he ought. It struck me immediately, "This is the thing; the very thing we have wanted so long. I called together all the leaders of the classes (as we used to term them and their companies) and desired that each would make a particular enquiry into the behaviour of those he saw weekly. They did so . . . As soon as possible the same method was used in London and all other places".

This structure gave people a link with the whole work. It cemented the work together, and gave it a durability, as well as protection, so essential to young converts. Fitzgerald says, "If it had not been for the Class Meeting, Methodism would have been a rope of sand."

And yet we must keep the essential point in mind, that it was the spirit of the class-meeting which intensified its value. It was the fellowship which the class-meeting symbolised that united the work.

Structures in themselves are of no lasting value, once bereft of the inner spirit in which they had their birth.

## HOUSES FOR WORSHIP

The Baldwin Street and Nicholas Street Societies in Bristol were growing rapidly. Accommodation was becoming altogether inadequate. Wesley was on the lookout for something new. There was a long strip of land between the Horsefair, and Broadmead which contained a garden. The property, including a little tenement, was owned by a William Lyne and occupied by one called Fisher. After seeking some advice Wesley ventured. He bought the property on May 9. The following Saturday the foundation stone was laid and the building was commenced. The step was providential, because certain events necessitated Wesley's departure from Baldwin Street. On June 3 we read the following account in the Journal.

"In the morning (preached) to about six thousand persons . . . In the afternoon at Rose-Green, to I believe eight or nine thousand. In the evening, not being permitted to preach in Baldwin Street, we met in the shell of our new society-room. The scripture which came in course to be explained was "Marvel not if the world hate you". We sang

"Arm of the Lord, awake, awake!
Thine own immortal strength put on!"

And God, even our own God, gave us His blessing.

The building was to be known as the New Room. It came about as a result of circumstances beyond Wesley's control. He had no intention to set up buildings in opposition to the Church of England. He could not have seen the outcome of these small beginnings. J.S. Simon says:- "He did not know that, so far as the Church of England was concerned, he had reached the 'parting of the ways' and was advancing on the path that would lead to the formation of one of the greatest Protestant churches in the world".

It would seem that Wesley had no intention of becoming responsible for the erection and running of the new establishment. He originally vested responsibility for this with eleven trustees. However when bills began to accumulate, Wesley requested financial assistance from Whitefield and the friends at London.

They only consented to support the work on the condition that the trustees be relieved of their responsibility, and Wesley take the entire responsibility upon his own shoulders.

This course was followed, and became the precedent of nearly all the chapels built in later years. The property was vested in himself until by the Deed of Declaration, he transferred it to the Legal Conference.

It is of further interest in this context to note that the debts referred to in the account of the class meeting were those incurred on the "New Room" building. The "penny a week" giving, envied by some notable students of Methodism, was the origin of freewill giving. The building projects rested on the generosity and love in the hearts of the people. It has been said, "The financial bedrock of Methodism is the "penny a week, shilling a quarter," a method of systematic liberality which originated at Bristol."

## SCHOOLS

Susanna Wesley's emphasis upon a good education for her children was perpetuated in John's ministry.

Whitefield's desire to provide schooling for the miners' children is evidenced in his laying a foundation stone on April 2, just before leaving the Kingswood area. Griffith Jones was already providing "Circulating Schools" in Wales, as we noted in a previous chapter. Something after a similar pattern was envisaged by Whitefield.

It was Wesley who carried the project through to its conclusion. Building commenced on June 26, after his return from London.

Education had been initiated at the Baldwin Street Society. It was also an integral part of the new room complex in the Horsefair. It was known for a time as "The New School-House in the Horsefair".

Four masters and a mistress were employed for the instruction of the children. In addition early morning and late evening classes were convened for the education of the older people.

Wesley saw a vital link between spiritual and week-day education of the older people.

He wanted to unite the pair so long disjoined; knowledge and vital piety. He was very successful and deserves to be "placed among the pioneers of popular education in England".

Richard Green the historian said that the spiritual movement led by Wesley 'gave the first impulse to our popular education'.

# NEW VENTURES IN LONDON

On June 11 1739 we find Mr. Wesley proceeding to London. His presence was imperatively required to help settle disturbing circumstances at the Fetter Lane Society. Some members advocated separation from the Church of England, believing that such a connection imposed too many restraints upon them. The leading protagonist, a man called Shaw, advocated the right of the laity to baptize and administer the Lord's Supper. Furthermore he propounded the belief that individual Christians were inspired, and had the right to interrupt meetings on the pretext that they had a message from God which must be delivered immediately.

Charles Wesley, the leader of the Society, set himself resolutely against Shaw and his supporters. In the providence of God the evil character of all this agitation was revealed.

A famous prophetess, who was influencing leading men in the Society, was found to be living immorally. The eyes of many were opened and at this perilous time, Wesley was implored to return to London. He arrived in London on June 13.

Though he only tarried five days before returning to Bristol, a number of eventful happenings took place. He met his mother whom he had not seen for a year. She received a first-hand account of his testimony.

Some misunderstandings were cleared up regarding his experience and thereafter she became a most ardent supporter of Methodism.

That evening the administrative ability of Wesley was amply displayed in the resolving of the Society's problems. Some were expelled, others were humbled, and sin was exposed.

God moved in a time of blessing upon the people, such as had not been known since the memorable New Year love-feast held there.

The outstanding event of the visit was when Wesley took his place as a field-preacher in London.

On June 14, he accompanied his friend George Whitefield,

who was still in London, to Blackheath. Twelve or fourteen thousand people were assembled. One can imagine Wesley's astonishment when Mr. Whitefield insisted that he preach the sermon. In his Journal he says, "I did preach (though nature recoiled) on my favourite subject, "Jesus Christ who of God is made unto us wisdom righteousness, sanctification and redemption."

Strikingly, he comments, "I was greatly moved with compassion for the rich that were there . . . Some seemed to attend, while others drove away in their coaches from so uncouth a preacher".

Perhaps he was reliving his previous experience with the upper society during his visit to the City of Bath. Of that encounter with the celebrated King of Bath, Beau Nash, and the ensuing disdain of the gentry, most people are well acquainted. Speaking to some fashionably but inquisitive ladies he said:- "I do not expect that the rich and great should want either to speak with me, or to hear me; for I speak the plain truth; a thing you hear little of and do not desire to hear". - June 5, 1739.

Regardless of their reaction the common people heard the Word and came back for more of the same preaching. The following Sunday at seven in the morning in Upper Moorfields six to seven thousand assembled and heard Wesley preach again on Isaiah 55 v.1 "Ho! everyone that thirsteth, come ye to the waters!" They were respectable people in general, that is when we compare them with the evening congregation. Across London on Kennington Common a vast crowd of fifteen thousand were gathered. The text was pungent and simple, "Look unto me, and ye be saved all the ends of the earth".

Leslie Church furnishes a graphic account of the populace in that district.

"Here you will find the rag-tag and bob-tail of London town. Here sooner or later you may come across all the pimps, and procurers, the pickpockets and vagabonds, who haunt the darker streets of the city at nights. An unsavoury place . . . For the first time in their lives they dare to wonder if God cares".

Wesley made his return journey to Bristol on the 18 June, thus spending a mere five days at the Metropolis. But they were eventful days. The seed bed was laid for a famous field of spiritual influence before many months were to elapse.

It is worth noting in relation to this visit to London that Mr. Wesley recorded one of the great statements of his life and ministry. It comes in his sometime previous reply of March 20, to James Harvey, a member of the original Holy Club. Harvey questioned Wesley's right and etiquette, (according to church principles), to minister to souls in another minister's parish. Wesley's reply, which he records in full in his Journal of June 11, 1739, makes quite clear how Wesley was thinking as he journeyed to the city. What may seem a rebuke to his longtime friend, is only fully appreciated in the context and spirit of the correspondence.

"Permit me to speak plainly. If by Catholic principles you mean any other than Scriptural they weigh nothing with me. I allow no other rule, whether of faith or practice, than the Holy Scriptures. But on Scriptural principles I do not think it hard to justify whatever I do. God in Scripture, commands me, according to my power, to instruct the ignorant, reform the wicked, to confirm the virtuous. Man forbids me to do this in another's parish that is, in effect not to do it at all: seeing I have now no parish of my own, nor probably ever shall. Whom then shall I hear, God or man? . . . Suffer me now to tell you my principles in this matter".

"I LOOK UPON ALL THE WORLD AS MY PARISH; thus far I mean, that in whatever part I am, I judge it meet, right, and my bounden duty, to declare to all that are willing to hear, the glad tidings of salvation".

Yes indeed, from brickyard or pithead, horse-fair in Bristol, fashionable Bath, Moorfields or Kennington Common it was all the same to John Wesley. He was going to those who needed him - to those who needed him most.

## AN OPERATIONS BASE ESTABLISHED

The period covering the final six months of 1739 are marked

by growing difficulties. As the Societies grew, so did the opposition.

Wesley's attacks upon the extreme doctrine of predestination aroused the hostility of various members both in Bristol and London.

There was a growing tendency to split from the established church; something Wesley strongly opposed.

A potential severance between Wesley and the Societies was forming since both were becoming more at variance as the days proceeded.

The winter of 1739-40 was approaching. It was imperative that some shelter be found for the crowds who attended the field meetings.

By November Wesley had returned yet again to London. His friend, Mr. Whitefield had sailed to America three months previously. Charles had taken charge of the Bristol work at the same time.

Fetter Lane Society was now in a critical condition. Moravian teaching was undermining Wesley's influence and ministry. Wesley sought to pour oil on troubled waters, but it was to no avail.

It was on Sunday, November 11, at eight in the morning when Mr. Wesley preached to a congregation of five or six thousand people. The place is not indicated but in all probability it was Upper Moorfields.

Leaving Upper Morfields in a northerly direction was a narrow thoroughfare, leading to open country between Old Street and Islington. The pathway passed a shattered ruins known as the "Old Foundery". It was here the king's cannon were cast, until the place was wrecked by an explosion in 1716. After twenty three years of desolation at five in the evening, Wesley preached in the old ruins. Writing in 1744 Wesley gives account of that historic day in London Methodism.

"In November 1739, two gentlemen, then unknown to me (Mr. Ball and Mr. Watkins) came and desired me, once and again, to preach in a place called the Foundery near Moorfields. With much reluctance I at length complied. I was soon after pressed to take that place into my own hands. Those who were most earnest therein lent me the purchase-money, which was one hundred and fifteen pounds".

It seems from this event that preparatory steps were being taken towards a final separation from the Fetter Lane Religious Society.

This great Methodist preaching and teaching centre served the work for thirty eight years before being superceded by City Road Chapel.

Leslie Church adds a very nostalgic paragraph to his account of the complex and its ministry.

"The old pulpit, which Wesley first used in the Foundery, now stands in the beautiful Chapel of Richmond College. One remembers experiencing a twinge of disappointment at discovering it was made of rough deal and elm. The feeling was momentary. No rare timber would have been so fitting. It was a field-preacher's pulpit after all!"

## A NEW SOCIETY

Wesley left for the West again on November 12. At Wycombe he prayed and conversed with two ministerial friends, John Gambold and a man called Robson. They compiled a six point agreement, which one can readily see, was to become in later years, a blue-print for Methodism.

"To meet yearly at London, if God permit, on the eve of Ascension Day".

"To fix then the business to be done the ensuing year; where, when and by whom".

"To meet quarterly there, as many as can; viz. on the second Tuesday in July, October, January and April".

"To send a monthly account to one another of what God hath done in each of our stations".

"To enquire whether Mr. Hall, Sympson, Rogers, Ingham, Hutchins, Kinchin, Stonehouse, Cannick, Oxlee and Brown will join us herein".

"To consider whether there be any others of our spiritual friends who are able and willing to do so".

So their intention was to form some kind of association distinct from those which were already in existence. The representation at meetings was to be composed of clergy and laymen. However, according to Mr. Simon, "the Wycombe scheme was never carried out".

Wesley's final visit to London in that year, runs from December 19, to January 3, 1740.

One supremely important event transpired during those days. The Journal record states on 24 December:- "After spending part of the night at Fetter Lane, I went to a smaller company, where also we exhorted one another with hymns and spiritual songs, and poured out our hearts to God in prayer".

The meeting place is not referred to, but by 1740 a new Society was meeting regularly at the Foundery. It was under the control of John Wesley, and distinct from the Fetter Lane Society. The formal termination with Fetter Lane came in July 1740.

We must, at this point, record the familiar words in the history of the work of the Methodists in London city.

"In the latter end of the year 1739 eight or ten persons came to me in London, who appeared to be deeply convinced of sin, and earnestly groaning for redemption. They desired (as did two or three more the next day) that I would spend some time with them in prayer,and advise them how to flee from the wrath to come; which they saw continually hanging over their heads. That we might have more time for this great work, I appointed a day in which we might all come together every week, namely on Thursday, in the evening ... This was the rise of the United Society, first in London and then in other places".

This account was written in May 1744 and the communication was entitled "The Nature, Design and General Rules of the United Societies in London, Bristol, Kingswood, Newcastle-upon-Tyne."

The obvious conclusions here are that no formal 'Rules' were drawn up for over three years. Thus there was no elaborate organisation as in the Religious Societies. The primary condition was a desire to flee from the wrath to come and be saved from their sins.

Perhaps Wesley did not perceive at this point in his life, that the circumstance which had brought about this new society, namely, a desire for severance from the church on the part of the Religious Society, was in effect going to recur by the very formation of his new society.

Surely the one condition of membership already stated, was going to sweep into the arms of the United Societies, multitudes, who had neither connection with, nor love for the Church of England. That is the very thing which did transpire, and as we now know, precipitated serious problems for Wesley in later years.

The other matter of interest is the inclusion of Newcastle-upon-Tyne. Thus we have, by 1744, Wesley's key centres of evangelism. They were great frontier positions of those early days. Yet all along the connecting travel routes, he established a multiplicity of preaching centres.

Before continuing our pursuit of the northerly road we would do well to reflect on the previous twelve months. Such a pageant of victory and blessing! Multitudes led to the saving grace of God, and true religion established in two great population centres of the eighteenth century England.

Matthew Lelievre made the observation that "this memorable year, 1739, spent by Wesley in self-consuming toil, saw the foundations of Methodism laid at many points simultaneously: London, Bristol, Kingswood. Wales had heard the word from these ardent missionaries, and the revival had begun to assume a form of solid stability."

If Wesley at this time had attained a clearer conception of the grandeur of the work set before him, he had already also good reason to calculate on its success.

## UNFURLING THE BANNER IN THE NORTH

The third key centre in the early history of Methodism was Newcastle-upon-Tyne. After a year of constant activity between London and Bristol which also saw an increase of hostility to the work of the evangelists, a variety of circumstances indicated that it was time to go North. This led him to the industrial heartland in May 1742.

## PROVIDENTIAL CIRCUMSTANCES

John Nelson was one of the first preachers whom God raised up to assist Wesley. He was a Yorkshire stone-mason who had come to saving knowledge of Christ. This had taken place when he heard Wesley preach in London in 1739. He returned to Birstal, the town of his birth. The simple warm hearted preaching along with the piety of his life, moved many to trust the Lord. He wrote to Mr. Wesley, seeking advice. The relative reply informed him that Mr. Wesley would visit him shortly

In addition to this, the countess of Huntingdon, a lady of nobility and wealth, who had given great support to the Methodist cause, corresponded with Mr. Wesley. She, along with her husband and Miss Fanny Cooper, lived at Donnington. Miss Cooper who was dying of consumption, greatly desired to see Mr. Wesley. An urgent plea reached Wesley in mid-May.

Sister Cooper was at the point of death. Wesley set out immediately, arriving on May 22nd to find her scarcely alive. He spent three days at the stately home before leaving for Birstal.

It should be said also that the Countess had for quite some time carried a great burden for the miners, at Newcastle. She had encouraged Wesley on different occasions to attend this spiritually deprived people. Surely what the Lord had done for the Kingswood men, he could do for the Northern men as well!

## FIRST-FRUITS AT BIRSTAL

Wesley reached Birstal on 26 May 1742. He was warmly received by Nelson. How pleasantly surprised he was by what he saw there:- "Many of the greatest profligates in all the county were now changed. Their blasphemies were turned to praise. Many of the most abandoned drunkards were now sober, many Sabbath-breakers remember the Sabbath day to keep it holy. The whole town wore a new face. Such a change did God work by the artless testimony of one plain man! And from thence his word sounded forth to Leeds, Wakefield, Halifax, and all the West-Riding of Yorkshire."

Later in the day as Wesley preached about two miles away at Dewsbury Moor, two men, later to become stalwarts of Methodism in the area, trusted the Lord.

## NEWCASTLE-UPON-TYNE

On Friday 28 May, Wesley approached the city. He passed through the town and remarked afterward:- "I was surprised: So much drunkenness, cursing and swearing, (even from the mouths of little children) do I never remember to have seen and heard before in so small a compass of time. Surely this place is ripe for Him who "came not to call the righteous but sinners to repentance."

At seven in the morning along with a companion John Taylor, the following Sunday being the 30 May, he went to the poorest and most contemptible part of the town. They began by singing the hundredth Psalm. Three or four inquisitive people came to see what was taking place. The crowd increased to about five hundred and before Wesley finished preaching there were twelve to fifteen hundred listeners. They were eyeing the strange preacher with profound astonishment when at length he said, "If you desire to know who I am, my name is John Wesley. At five in the evening with God's help I design to preach here again".

True to his word, he arrived to find an extraordinary number of people assembled. The crowds at Moorfield and Kennington were not to be compared with this multitude.

From the summit to the base of the hillside they stood together. The preacher stood at its summit and preached on "I will heal their backsliding, I will love them freely". After concluding, the people pressed around him.

Out of pure love and kindness they almost trod him under foot. He could scarcely get back to his lodgings. They implored him to remain for some days. But as always, Wesley had a tight schedule. He must proceed to Bristol again. He set out at three in the morning and travelled eighty miles before sunset found him at Burroughbridge. Next evening he preached for two and a half hours at his planned destination.

Shortly after leaving Newcastle, his brother Charles arrived to continue the work. Before the end of the year John returned and devoted six weeks to evangelisation of the entire area. Nowhere had the reception been so cordial. In addition there were numerous conversions. Great power and deep conviction attended the meetings. People were smitten down under the agonies of soul anguish similar to some of the manifestations which had occurred in the Southern counties.

It was during this second visit that some ground was purchased on December 4. The foundation stone for the new building was laid on the 20th. Great crowds gathered and with twenty six shillings in hand the work was commenced. The projected cost of erecting the chapel with its adjoining school was seven hundred pounds. It was called "The Orphan House". The farewell sermon was preached to a vast crowd on the 30 December. They hung on every word, so that Wesley could not disengage himself without great difficulty. Seven weeks later he returned to supervise the building and on 25 March 1743 he preached his first message in the shell of the new building. His message was on "the rich man and Lazarus".

Telford writes of the centre there in a glowing account:- "It had a blessed history. Its school . . . provided for forty poor children. One of the first Sunday schools in the North with a thousand scholars met there; it had its Bible Society before the British and Foreign Bible Society was established. In its choir, one of the best in the country, the sons of Mr. Scott afterward the celebrated Lord Elden and Lord Stowell, were sometimes found. The colliers and keelmen of the district were so eager to hear the Wesleys that they would lie down on the benches after evening service and sleep till the hour for early morning preaching".

The description given by Mr. Church reveals at a glance how well adapted the Newcastle building was as a centre for the work in the north.

When it was completed the lower part was used as a chapel, fitted with pulpit and forms. Over the main building was a band room, and class-rooms. On the upper storey were apartments for the preachers and their families, and on the roof itself was a wooden hut, eleven feet square, which was called 'Mr. Wesley's study'.

It was right here in February 22nd 1743 that Mr. Wesley drew up his rules for his Societies, to which we have already made reference.

We have now identified the geographical structure of early Methodism. It is obvious that Wesley pursued, roughly, England's industrial development. He worked where the population was most concentrated. He constantly traversed the road from London to Newcastle - 270 miles, Newcastle to Bristol 320 miles, and Bristol to London 120 miles. Hulme says "The first four times he rode over that triangular area were in the sixteen months before May 1742 and August 1743, and twice in the depth of winter".

Dr. Fitchett makes the remark that around this triangle, with some smaller percentage being allowed for variation of activity, Wesley must have been as intimately acquainted as any city postman was with his daily rounds .

## THE FUTURE STRATEGY

It is not our design to follow laboriously every footstep of Wesley's great fifty year itineracy. But from 1744 when the first Methodist Conference convened in London we find the principle of his future action. There were six clergymen and four lay-preachers assembled on that memorable occasion at the Foundery.

At the conference the first issue was the regulation of doctrine, discipline and practice.

On the matter of association between the Church of England and the Societies they discussed at some length. Wesley did foresee the possibility of a cleavage in due course but it was not his design to precipitate such a division. That would come about at the instigation of state church action. He said:-

"We are persuaded that the body of our hearers will, even after our death, remain in the Church, unless they be thrust out. We believe, notwithstanding, either that they will be thrust out, or that they will leaven the whole church. "

That the latter did not transpire, we are now fully aware, and Wesley was moved by circumstances to make provision for the other and less welcome alternative.

A further question must be answered. What is the best way of spreading the Gospel? The answer reveals the leadership genius of John Wesley and is a blueprint for any successful progress in the work of the Lord for all time.

To go a little and a little from London, Bristol, St. Ives, Newcastle, or any other Society so a little leaven would spread with more effect and less noise, and help would always be at hand.

At this point we must pause in the onward march. Other forces combined to make the infant movement vibrant and strong. We have deliberately passed over them with a minimum of emphasis because they deserve a more distinct consideration.

# 5

# THE ANTHEMS OF PRAISE

While John Wesley rightly holds the position of prominence over his brother Charles, the work would never have been the same without Charles.

He was the one who took charge of the Fetter Lane Society after John departed for Bristol in 1739.

When John became busily engaged in itinerant preaching, Charles took the oversight of the Bristol work. In 1742 after John's departure from Newcastle-upon-Tyne it was his brother who arrived to a great and welcoming people.

He was an excellent preacher who had also suffered the same fate as his brother. The churches were closed against him and he made his debut in field preaching on 24 June 1739. It was at Moorfields in London before a crowd of ten thousand helpless sinners. His text was Matthew ch.11.v.28. After this venturing forth he records in his journal, "My load was gone, and all my doubts and scruples. God shone upon my path, and I knew this was His will concerning me."

From this time forth he preached with great saving effect to the assembled crowds wherever he went.

But he will pre-eminently be known as the sweet psalmist of Methodism. Methodism was the singing movement.

## ENGLAND IN SONG

The first words that met Charles Wesley's eyes when he turned to the Bible after his conversion were "He hath put a new song in my mouth".

The poetic streak in his father resided in him also. The harmony of grace found an outlet in his first post-conversion hymn. It characterises the spirit of early Methodism in its overflowing joy, and intense spiritual conviction,

"Where shall my wondering soul begin?
How shall I all to heaven aspire?
A slave redeemed from death and sin, A brand plucked from eternal fire,
How shall I equal triumphs raise,
Or sing my great Deliverer's praise"?

Here is a man breaking into the bright almost dazzling gleams of a new morning.

His later compositions "And can it be that I should gain" along with "Wrestling Jacob" published in 1742 were much more clearly thought out.

The lines of his great evangelical conversion were drawn in sharper focus by then. Yet for freshness, his first expression must maintain its superiority. Here is the questioning wonder of his heart, formed in the where and how of the stanza.

The second verse conveys the superlativeness of his experience over his scope of expressions.

"Oh how shall I the goodness tell,
Father, which Thou to me has show'd?
That I a child of wrath and hell,
I should be called a child of God!
Should know, should feel my sins forgiven,
Blest with this antepast of heaven"!

But ere long he makes his decision to confess his Saviour before men . . . It may be revolutionary. Let it be vulgar, unorthodox, foolish in the eyes of a sleeping ecclesiasticism! What he thereafter wrote is strikingly prophetic of the events less than a year hence when these men took to the fields with the glorious evangel.

> "Outcasts of men, to you I call,
> Harlots and publicans and thieves!
> He spreads His arms to embrace you all;
> Sinners alone His grace receives;
> No need of Him the righteous have,
> He came the lost the seek and save".

> "Call all ye Magdalens in lust,
> Ye ruffians fell in murders old;
> Repent and live: despair and trust:
> Jesus for you to death was sold!
> Though hell protest, and earth repine,
> He died for crimes like yours and mine".

In addition to those already mentioned, we have, in those early days such hymns as 'Come Holy Ghost all-quickening fire!' - 'Christ, whose glory fills the skies', 'Jesu lover of my soul', 'Oh for a thousand tongues to sing', and 'Earth rejoice our Lord is King'. One can only begin to imagine the impact upon England. The vast crowds assembled, exulting in a new-found faith, and singing with all their hearts!

## EXCLAMATIONS ABUNDANT

Ritual deadness has vanished with the emergence of Charles Wesley's hymns. A careful study of the lines reveals an important key to the spirit of early Methodism.

The hymns are permeated with exclamation marks. Line after line terminates with the wondering punctuation. George Findlay said:- "Perhaps the folk in those days were more lavish with them than is the fashion today. Or was it that the early Methodists had so much to exclaim about, so very much to make them want to shout"?

On average it has been computed that there are about two exclamations per hymn throughout the entire compilation, which reached about seven thousand three hundred hymns in total.

It may be concluded that if John was the reserved

administrator, Charles was the buoyant poet. Grace released the springs of joy, and life became an open-ended exclamation mark.

## EXTRAVAGANCE OF SPEECH

Charles employed polysyllabic words with undisguised delight. We have only to think of his 'inextinguishable blaze' in 'Oh Thou who camest from above'. A sample of others are: unutterable, unspeakable (employed regularly) incomprehensible, unfathomable, inseparably, and ecstatic. Remember that these were written for ordinary people - largely illiterate people! Yet in spite of the language they sang them.

Other regular words like amazing, wonderful, rapturous,and wondering, supplement the vast array of adjectives.

But Wesley's addiction appears in a small word 'all' along with its synonyms 'every' and 'whole'. Yes, this was a message for all men everywhere.

> "Oh for a trumpet voice,
> On all the world to call,
> To bid their hearts rejoice,
> In him who died for all!
> For all my Lord was crucified,
> For all, for all my Saviour died".

Findlay says, "Yes 'all' is a far reaching word most particularly suitable to the message Charles Wesley had to proclaim; it points in every direction, up and down, inwards and outwards".

He also extended the range of some twenty seven participles and adjectives ad infinitum by prefixing them with the word 'all'. A few examples will suffice: all-alluring, all-atoning, cleansing, creating and prevailing. Of the latter there is his all-glorious, gracious, perfect and victorious, alongside others.

## SCRIPTURAL CONCEPTS

Charles Wesley placed the fundamentals of the faith in

metre. His hymns are "steeped in scriptural thought".

No truth is too deep, no thought too lofty, no conception too subtle to elude the poet's grasp, and there are luminous expository, experimental hymns in which whole sermons and treatises are crystallised into beautiful and forceful expression.

Especially is this a fact in "And can it be" where a total of thirty six Scripture passages are verbally and definitely illustrated.

Rattenbury has expressed the view, and with ample justification, that "Charles Wesley's medium of expressing theology was in song".

## THE VITAL INFLUENCE

The voice of praise and song is no longer a revolution in the church. In Wesley's day it was in its infancy. Philip Doddridge and Isaac Watts had produced a number of great hymns around the close of the seventeenth century. In 1737 John Wesley had a little book of hymns published for the people in Georgia. The Moravian people knew something of the joy of song, but it was the soul-stirring impress on Charles Wesley's hymns which gave dynamism to Methodism. Leslie Church said:- "They are not just solemn paraphrases of scripture - they have their own vitality, they are alive, your heart dances as you sing, or it is bowed with shame, or again it rises up on wings to the very throne of God".

Let us also remember that the use of the hymn in church was confined to the Dissenters. Anything apart from the Psalms of David was seriously handicapped before it even started. How then do we account for the immediate vogue which they achieved? Dr. Frederick Wiseman says that "since their use was confined to meetings which were not regarded as usurping the functions of public worship, they did not transgress the laws of church order".

In addition, the people who sang them were, by and large, the unchurched masses. They had no scruples about church polity! Here were hymns with feeling; with life as well as biblical truth. The tunes were suited to the day and thus the great congregation could thrill to the occasion. Creamer declared:-"Had not Charles Wesley been providentially led to write sacred poetry, there would have been a serious deficiency in Methodism; its progress would not have been as rapid, nor its influences so extensive. It could not have been so serviceable in kindling and sustaining the devotional spirit in the great congregation, or in aiding the religious exercises of the family and the duties of the closet. It could not have contributed so largely to alarm the careless and impenitent sinner; to encourage and assist the sincere seeker of salvation; to comfort the Christian believer amid all the difficulties and discouragements of his way; to urge him on to the hot pursuit and attainment of high degrees of holiness; to administer consolation to the subjects of pain and affliction; and to enable the dying Christian to meet the last enemy with composure and fortitude, triumphing through his great Redeemer."

The only serious rival to Wesley was Watts. And yet they were complementary in their great capabilities. It has been said that Watts possessed a catholicity of sentiment, breadth of treatment and smoothness of language, whereas Wesley who was more often bounded by the horizon of the Methodist awakening was characterized by greater strength of wing, vigour of stroke and daring in flight.

We humbly praise God for both men. Their ministry is perpetuated to this day. The acceptance of the compositions of Charles Wesley encompasses all nations and has over passed all ecclesiastical boundaries. The Church universal has been challenged, inspired and blessed beyond measure. Leslie Church made the pungent statement that:- "No one can understand the real meaning of Methodism who is not prepared to read carefully the hymns of Charles Wesley, and try to understand their vital message to an eighteenth century England, whose religious outlook had become dim and impersonal".

Bernard Manning, the noted Congregationalist, issued a salutory warning to Methodism in the year 1932.

"You talk much, and you talk rightly of the work

Methodism does for the world and for the universal Church; but your greatest - incomparably your greatest - contribution to common heritage of Christendom is in Wesley's hymns . . . In them you have something unique . . . I implore you then . . . to keep that good thing committed peculiarly to your charge. In Wesley's hymns . . . you have what only you understand and what (I fear) you no longer think it worth while to understand".

Did he perceive a contemptuous element taking hold of the church? Was familiarity breeding a people without the soul of their founders? What if Wesley were to return again and survey the scene? Here are his directions to the people called Methodist.

"Suit the time to the words. Avoid complex tunes, which it is scarcely possible to sing with devotion . . . Sing no anthems. Do not suffer the people to sing too slow . . . Exhort every one in the congregation to sing - not one in ten only".

These exhortations are worthy of consideration. This is the way to save our services from formality.

While the evangelists traversed the land, the people whom they won to the Saviour were taught the melodies of grace. The mines were transformed from cess-pools of sin to cathedrals of song. The common theme, learned by all, whether in Bristol, London, Newcastle-upon-Tyne or anywhere else the evangel arrived, welded the hearts of the people together. It was the church singing triumphantly and extolling the Lamb upon His heavenly throne.

# 6

# A NEW ORDER OF PREACHERS

The lives and ministries of Wesley's early itinerant preachers formed the structural marrow of Methodism. Without them, the work would never have attained the heights of success which it experienced.

It is obvious that the phenomenal growth of the Methodist movement even in 1739 alone, made it impossible for Whitefield and the Wesley brothers to cover all the work. God in His providence again raised up a new order of preachers from among the people. They were men, in some instances, possessed of extraordinary power and heroic spirit. Their appearance on the scene is all the more interesting in that apart from any interconnection between them they appeared simultaneously in different parts of the country.

## THE RELUCTANT WESLEY

It must be stressed that John Wesley had no part in the establishment of this arm of outreach. After his conversion, all the stubborn prejudices of a high churchman remained with him. A layman preaching was tantamount to sacrilege. That was the sole right bequeathed to ordained ministers. Yet the irony of history is that Methodism engaged the services of more lay-preachers than any other denomination.

But circumstances demanded an answer. He must have

associates. There were a few faithful clergymen but they were tied to their parish work. As the wave swept onward they became afraid of the future result. Wesley knew only too well that the base must be broader than one or two individuals. His adversaries realised full well too that if anything should happen to Wesley himself, the figure-head would have disappeared. The slender thread of one life might not hold out for too long. With all the work hinged upon him the demise would come shortly after his death.

There were no successors and there were very few friends. They must be taken from among the army of new converts.

## INTRODUCING THE NEW PRACTICE - HOWELL HARRIS

As early as 1735 Howell Harris, to whom we have already made reference, had engaged in this vocation.

He had been denied episcopal ordination on three occasions. Spiritual resolution motivated him to found thirty private prayer societies, and in succeeding months he became God's instrument in the gracious awakening in Wales. Dr. Tyerman has furnished a brief account of the circumstances of his ministry.

"It was a curious fact, not generally noticed, that the first lay-preacher in the great Methodist movement, was Howell Harris. He commenced preaching in Wales just when the Wesleys and Ingham commenced in Georgia; and before Wesley reached Bristol in 1739, had been the means of a most glorious work being wrought in the neighbouring principality. Harris first commenced visiting from house to house in his own native parish, and in neighbouring ones. The people flocked together and almost without knowing it he began to preach . . . Thus Howell Harris was an itinerant preacher at least a year and a half before Whitefield and Wesley were; and as the brave hearted herald of hundreds more who were to follow him, he met the fiercest persecutions with an undaunted soul and an unflinching face".

## JOHN CENNICK

In the annals of English Methodist lay-preachers this gracious man of God takes the primary position. Wesley makes the assertion that Joseph Humphrys was the first to assist him in England in 1738.

Tyerman comments that "Wesley, who was now in his eighty eighth year, was mistaken and it was 1740 because Humphrys preached at the Foundery. In any case if it was prior to Wesley's going to Bristol it must have been within the Moravian context when he preached".

John Cennick had arrived at Kingswood from Reading on June 11 1739. He was there at Wesley's invitation, to take charge of the school now being built for the colliers' children. On the following day a crowd of five hundred were assembled under a sycamore tree to hear the word of God preached.

The expected preacher did not arrive. Wesley was out of Bristol at the time. What was to be done? The people appealed to the stranger from Reading. He reluctantly consented, and said, "The Lord bore witness with my words, insomuch that many believed in that hour". He preached the following day and then twice on the Sunday following. John Wesley returned to Bristol on June 18.

After he preached at the New Room on his return a significant interview transpired. Howell Harris and John Wesley met for the first time at Wesley's lodgings. Both men fell upon their knees before God. Howell Harris relates the moment, "He (Wesley) was greatly enlarged in prayer for me and for all Wales".

Surely John Wesley's prejudice was greatly removed by the report which the young Welsh evangelist gave to him. It would seem so because when Wesley and Cennick met, instead of forbidding him, as some desired, the great man encouraged him.

Thus encouraged he preached constantly in Kingswood and in the neighbouring villages for the next eighteen months, and sometimes supplied Wesley's place in Bristol when he was absent, preaching in other towns.

## THOMAS MAXFIELD

It is often reported that Thomas Maxfield was the first lay-preacher of Methodism. The foregoing facts discount this, and also the knowledge that Maxfield was not converted until May 1739 supports the matter.

It was toward the end of that year, when Wesley was in Bristol, that Maxfield appeared in his new role at the Foundery in London. The strange thing is Wesley's reaction to the news that Thomas Maxfield had turned preacher. The churchmanship in Wesley revived. He hastened back to London to put an end to this practice. He arrived only to be met by his mother who cautioned him as to his intended line of action.

"John, you know what my sentiments have been. You cannot suspect me of favouring readily anything of this kind. But take care what you do with respect to that young man, for he is as truly called of God to preach as you are. Examine what have been the fruits of his preaching and hear him also yourself".

Wesley listened, watched and considered. His prejudices may have been stubborn but they yielded to the facts. There had been fruit and that was the end of controversy. "It is the Lord, let Him do what seemeth Him good."


## JOHN NELSON

Reference has been made already to this remarkable servant of God. He himself said he would rather be hanged on a tree than go to preach.

But preach he did by popular demand. The crowds gathered around him and hung upon his words. The Spirit of God wrought upon individuals, and every week the Society was increased numerically. When Wesley did eventually arrive in 1742, both men sat down together and discussed the work. The issue was settled for Wesley. A new order of helpers was being raised up by the Spirit for the great work.

Tyerman said "Wesley could not, durst not, forbid an

increase to the staff, because the added workers had not been trained in colleges . . . No doubt he would have preferred the employment of clerics like himself; but in the absence of such, he was driven to adopt the measure which we think the salvation of his system, and, in some respects, its glory."

## THEIR PERSECUTORS AND PRIVATIONS

It would be difficult to find a more dedicated group of preachers. They travelled around on the faithful horses which were indispensible to their labours. Thomas Olivers rode one horse for twenty five years. It covered about one hundred thousand miles. All this, from a beast which had initially cost only five pounds!

When these men arrived in the towns and villages they often experienced hard and long struggles with the mobs. Sometimes stoned, other times cast into ponds, often beaten with sticks and on occasions put into the cells for vagrants, they counted their troubles light in the sense of duty and love which compelled them. Wesley loved this heroic band as these words indicate:- "I pray you, for what pay could we procure men to do this service? To be always ready to go to prison or to death"?

They also lived on a meagre livelihood. Their saddle bags contained a scanty wardrobe and some Methodist tracts or books for the circuits.

Highwaymen passed them without interference. There was nothing worth molesting them for anyway.

John Downes' wife possessed one sixpence at the time of her husband's death. John Janes' clothes barely sufficed to pay the thirty-seven shillings and three pence required to cover his funeral expenses.

Initially circuits provided for the preacher, but there was no allowance for his wife. In course of time a four shillings per week allowance was granted for the wife and a sovereign each quarter for each child. In 1752 it was decided to give them twelve pounds a year, in order to buy clothes and other necessities.

## THE GUIDING PRINCIPLES

It might be wondered if Wesley had any criterion by which he accepted these men into his work. Were they just picked at random? Did they apply to Wesley? What standard was required of them?

Perhaps we see the prototypes in the apostles. They were unlearned and ignorant men but the people took knowledge of them that they had been with Jesus, (Acts 4.v.13.)

Wesley's preachers were men of God. They were consumed with a passion for the lost souls of men. They were motivated by a spring of divine love.

Nevertheless there were some fundamental essentials required.

## THEIR QUALIFICATIONS

It was the various conferences in early Methodism which formulated the rules as follows:-

"Do they know in whom they have believed? Have they the love of God in their hearts? Do they desire and seek nothing but God?

Have they the gifts (as well as grace) for the work?

Have they success? Do they not only so speak as generally either to convince or affect the hearts but have any received remission of sins by their preaching? A clear and lasting sense of the love of God?

As long as these three marks undeniably occur in any we allow him to be called of God to preach. These we receive as sufficient reasonable evidence that he is moved thereto by the Holy Ghost".

## THE TWELVE RULES

When a man was accepted into the work he received his now famous code "Twelve Rules of a Helper" which had been compiled by Wesley. The are ideal for the Methodist preacher to this day.

Be diligent. Never be unemployed a moment. Never while away time; neither spend any more time at any place than is strictly necessary.

Be serious. Let your motto be, 'Holiness unto the Lord'. Avoid all lightness, jesting and foolish talking.

Converse sparingly and cautiously with women, particularly with young women.

Take no steps towards marriage without first consulting with your brethren.

Believe evil of no one unless you see it done, take heed how you credit it. Put the best construction on everything. You know the judge is always supposed to be on the prisoner's side.

Speak evil of no one, else your word especially would eat as doth a canker. Keep your thoughts within your own breast, till you come to the person concerned.

Tell everyone what you think wrong in him, and that plainly, as soon as may be, else it will fester in your heart. Make all haste to cast the fire out of your bosom.

Do not affect the gentleman.

Be ashamed of nothing but sin. Not of fetching wood or drawing water; not of cleaning your own shoes or your neighbours.

Be punctual. Do everything exactly at the time . . .

You have nothing to do but save souls. Therefore spend and be spent in this work, And go always, not only to those who want you, but to those who want you most . . Act in all things, not according to your own will, but as a son in the gospel . . ."

In addition to these requirements, Wesley's men were to be readers of good books. They were to employ about five hours in every twenty four in such an exercise. If they did not possess any, Mr. Wesley provided them with five pounds worth of reading material.

These self-taught and Spirit-led men became equipped and capable of expounding truth in a remarkable manner.

## THE MESSAGE PREACHED

It is a well-known fact that the Wesley's and Whitefield had a very distinct and differing emphasis in their preaching. It was a fundamental and doctrinal difference. The Wesley's gave expression to evangelical Arminianism while George Whitefield embraced Calvinism. Wesley's emphasis is embodied in his sermon on Free Grace given in June 1739. It was published freely along with a thirty six stanza hymn composed by Charles. Whitefield preached on the absolute decrees at the Foundery in the presence of a number of thousands of people, Charles Wesley sitting by his side.

The strife of opinion was protracted and grave. There was a final rupture by March 1741. Cennick, Harris, Lady Huntingdon and others supported Whitefield and formed the basis of the Calvinistic Methodist Church and the Countess of Huntingdon's Connexion.

Wesley made attempt to convene a conference in August 1743 with his brother, in the company of Whitefield and the Moravians. This attempt to heal the doctrinal breach fell through, as the parties mentioned did not feel inclined to participate. Charles Spurgeon said, "Never were Wesley and Whitefield divided in heart though they were divided in other respects".

"These two men of God were much better apart, to go forth and preach their own views as they believed them, without quarrelling; for I am sure that if they had attempted to remain together they must have quarrelled . . . I do verily believe that there was twice as much good done as there could have been, had they constantly acted together".

Subsequent to the organisational separation the Wesleyan doctrine became more sharply focussed. The articles and homilies of the Church of England were given an Arminian emphasis. They preached with ceaseless repetition on universal depravity, universal redemption, the assurance of salvation, the virtue of public testimony and holiness of heart.

The five universals of Methodism were constantly upon their lips.

"All men need to be saved".

"All men may be saved".

"All men may know themselves saved".

"All men should declare their salvation".

"All men should perfect holiness in the fear of the Lord".
How were they to present their message?

Mr. Wesley gave them some very basic guidelines. They were to invite, to convince, to offer Christ and to build up; and to do this in some measure in every sermon. They were to choose the plainest texts, suit the subject to the audience, keep close to the main theme, avoid rambling, spiritualising and allegorising too much.

The steadfastness and enthusiasm with which these preachers went forth, ought to kindle the flame of zeal and devotion in any heart in our own time. They were soldier-heroes of which any work would be justly proud.

President Theodore Roosevelt commenting on the Methodist Revival said:- "If we are to advance in our conquest over the hidden forces of nature, it must be by developing strength in virtue, and virtue in strength, by breeding, and training men who shall be both good and strong, both gentle and valiant - men who scorn wrong-doing, and who, at the same time, have both the courage and the strength to strive mightily for the right".

The men who supported Wesley in the awakening were just such men as Roosevelt was referring to in this extract.

# 7

# THE PARISH BOUNDARIES EXTENDED

Wesley was in the Pauline succession in that the great apostle professed his willingness "to preach the gospel in the regions beyond."

He was now the great itinerant whose travels took him to Wales in 1739. He was happy to commit the work there to the continued ministry of Howell Harris. England was being steadily conquered for the Lord. It was time to enlarge the coast of the labours. It will be of interest to some to consider the establishment of Methodism in the remaining principalities within these isles, namely Ireland and Scotland.

## TAKING ROOT IN IRELAND

Some very fine and extensive accounts of Wesley's work in Ireland have been produced. The classic three volume work of C. H. Crookshank is one of the most exhaustive. It ought to be remembered that Ireland has been identified with Methodism from its inception. Mr. William Morgan, one of the first four members of the Oxford Holy Club, came from Ireland. In 1738 George Whitefield landed at County Clare, having been driven to the coast by strong winds, during his homeward voyage from America. He passed through Limerick, where he preached. Three days later he arrived in Dublin where he spent five days and preached twice in two very crowded city churches.

John Cennick arrived in Dublin by requests in 1746 and preached to a little group with Baptist connections.

The first Methodist preacher to come to Ireland was Thomas Williams. His ministry was signally blessed as he preached in the open air. Premises were acquired with accommodation for a hundred people, with ample space in an adjoining yard for four or five times that number to stand and hear the word of God.

When he sent an account of the rapid growth in the work to Mr. Wesley, the great man came without delay to see for himself. He arrived on August 9, 1747. He was entertained by Mr. Zunell, a wealthy Huguenot businessman, who had joined with the Methodists.

Mr. Wesley preached to large crowds on the following day. The prospects looked so favourable that Wesley felt there was potential for more extensive growth than in the London Society.

He wrote to Mr. Ebenezer Blackwell, a friend in England as follows, "I have found a home in this strange land. I am in Mr. Zunell's just as at the Foundery . . . For natural sweetness of temper, for courtesy and hospitality, I have never seen any people like the Irish. Indeed, all I converse with are only English people transplanted into another soil; and they are much amended by the removal, having left all the roughness and surliness behind them. They receive the Word of God with all gladness and readiness of mind".

Before returning to England two weeks later, Mr. Wesley examined all who desired to unite with the Society. He found two hundred and eighty members, many of whom appeared to be strong in faith.

In course of time the Methodists were assailed by angry mobs both Protestant and Papist. The fires of persecution were ignited, but in spite of the fury, the work increased daily and soon numbered three hundred and eighty members.

Mr. Trembath, who was at this time in charge of the Society, wrote to Wesley. "No one" said he, "is fit to be a preacher here who is not ready to die at any moment."

The work was greatly strengthened by the presence and ministry of Charles Wesley who arrived on September 9th and remained until March 20th.

At the turn of the year there were about seven Methodist preachers working in Ireland. Three were in the city of Dublin and others were establishing a bridgehead for the Lord in the midland counties.

At Tyrrell's Pass there was a remarkable work. People were hungry for the Word of God. Swearers, drunkards, Sabbath breakers, thieves, and villains were transformed.

"Near one hundred are joined to the Society and following hard after God," was Charles' account at the end of January 1748.

## WESLEY'S FIRST TOUR

John Wesley returned to the island on March 8th. Three weeks later he travelled with two companions to Philipstown, Tullamore, Clara, Moate, and eventually arrived at Athlone. Many Roman Catholic people attended the open-air meetings and listened attentively. At Tyrrell's Pass God signally blessed the ministry of the Word. He returned to Dublin on April 15, and preached to an abundance of people at Edenderry. But Wesley was thirsty for a move of the Spirit! He said, "There is not such a work as I look for. I see nothing yet but drops before a shower."

Two weeks later he set forth again from Dublin for the open doors at Birr, Ballyboy, Mountmellick and Aughrim. Some insurrections were mounted by the Roman Catholics, urged on by their clergy. The word of the gospel continued to be preached.

During one of the services a hearer cried out, shaking his head very wisely, "Aye, he is a Jesuit - that's plain." To which a priest who happened to overhear the comment said, "No, he is not. I would to God he was."

Back in London again on June 2, 1748, some of the preachers from Ireland attended the Conference. The country was divided into four areas or circuits consisting of Dublin,

Tullamore, Tyrrell's Pass, and Athlone. Two converts from the first twelve months labour were received into the preaching fraternity.

During this year other brethren had moved to Cork. It was ripe for the gospel. A work was established in Bandon, where a Mr. Murray, who had joined the Methodists set up home. Urgent calls were sent to Charles Wesley. He responded with whole-hearted endeavour and arrived, having preached on the course of travel at Tyrrell's Pass, Roscrea, Cashel, and Ballyboy.

The Sunday after his arrival at five in the morning, about one thousand persons "devoured every word with an eagerness beyond description."

That evening he preached to thousands upon thousands high and low, Protestant and Roman Catholic, who had waited for hours to hear the glad tidings of salvation.

Other towns and areas such as Passage West, Rathcormack, Bandon, and Kinsale were visited as well. Charles returned eventually to Dublin and set sail for England on October 8, a voyage which was both tempestuous and perilous. Shortly after his departure the Methodist cause in Cork was exposed to a vicious and protracted period of open hostility. People were cruelly persecuted and mobbed.

Their properties were, on various occasions, torn apart and burned with fire. The campaign appeared to have ample support from clergy and lawyers. Instead of bringing the hooligans to justice the Methodists were pillaried, and thus the ringleader's zeal was only intensified. One of the most prominent of these was a cruel individual named Nicholas Butler. His venom knew no restraint, but in process of time he suffered a major injury in the loss of an arm, and dragged out the remainder of his life in Dublin. In fact it was the charity of the Dublin Methodists that saved him from starvation.

The good seed of the Word was being widely sown in the country. Before leaving Ireland after his third visit in 1749, Wesley was able to record with great satisfaction that his workers had planted the work in Munster and Leinster.

Considerable numbers had been led to the Lord. This was within the first two years of Irish Methodism.

## SOME KEY PEOPLE IN IRISH METHODISM

It would be quite impossible and impracticable to produce a year by year account of eighteenth century Irish Methodism. F. C. Gill said, "Never since the days of St. Patrick had Ireland known such flaming evangelism, or greeted a more fervent apostle." Even the soldiers in the Athlone barracks felt he was superhuman.

John Wesley paid twenty one visits to Ireland, the last being in 1789, two years before his death. The total time period spent in Ireland embraced five and a half years of his public ministry. Was it worth the effort?

Wesley felt confident about the potential. In earlier years some of his London leaders expressed regret that he spent so much time in Ireland. Wesley replied, "Have patience and Ireland will repay you." These words were fulfilled in a very pleasant and abundant manner.

## THE PALATINE CONNEXION

Early in the eighteenth century a large number of people fled from the Palatinate on the Rhine.

The cruelty inflicted by Louis the Fourteenth drove them to emigrate to Ireland. They were mostly settled in Limerick, with a few in Kerry and Courtmatrix. The first contact with Methodist preaching was when Mr. Williams arrived in Limerick in 1749.

It reminded them of former days in Germany. Their hearts were stirred and the first to trust Christ was Philip Guier, the teacher of the German school at Ballingrane.

The blessing eventually came to Courtmatrix through a local woman who had gone to Limerick seeking legal help toward the settlement of a neighbourhood dispute. While at the city she found the Lord and brought back the Saviour to the settlement.

Following the steps of Wesley it becomes evident that he had a special place in his heart for these good people. He made regular trips to Limerick throughout the succeeding years. Who could have predicted the sequel to this association?

## BARBARA RUCKLE

To those not acquainted with early Methodism the name bears no significance. But oh what profound usefulness was to emanate from this life!

Barbara was born in Ballingrane in 1734. At eighteen years of age she joined the Methodists. She was a godly girl, if ever there was one in the area. The clear witness of the Spirit never left her during a long life.

She married Paul Heck; thereafter bearing what was to become a distinguished name in the annals of Methodism; **Barbara Heck**

## PHILIP EMBURY

Born in the same village as Barbara in 1728, he attended the school of which Philip Guier was the teacher. He heard Mr. Wesley preach in Limerick in 1752. The Spirit of God wrought conviction upon his heart, which eventually resulted in his salvation. He gives his own account of the momentous event. "On Christmas Day, being Monday 25 December 1752, the Lord shone into my soul, by a glimpse of His redeeming love, being an earnest of my redemption in Christ Jesus to whom be glory for ever and ever. Amen."

In the early 1760's a little group of people stood at the Custom-House quay in Limerick. They were saying their last farewell to the land of their birth, and setting sail for the new world, America.

In that group were Paul Heck and his wife, Barbara, along with Philip Embury. The latter two were destined in the providence of God to influence countless myriads to the paths of righteousness. The vessel that pushed away from the shore was carrying the germ from which sprang the Methodist Church of America. Indeed Barbara Heck became known as the Mother of American Methodism.

# THOMAS WALSH

No history of Methodism in Ireland is complete without mention of this great man. He had been won to Christ from Roman Catholicism, through hearing the glorious invitation "Come unto me all ye that labour...." from the lips of a Methodist lay-preacher at a Limerick street corner. God and salvation became powerful realities in his conscious being. He wrote of that event: "God and the things of the invisible world, of which I had only heard before by the hearing of the ear, appeared now in their true light as substantial realities. Faith gave me to see a reconciled God and an all-sufficient Saviour. The kingdom of God was within me. I drew water out of the wells of salvation. I walked and talked with God all the day long, whatsoever I believed to be His will I did with my whole heart. I could unfeignedly love them that hated me and pray for them that despitefully used and persecuted me. The commandments of God were my delight".

His communion with God was exceedingly intimate. He appeared to live in the realm of the celestial. It was said that "he walked through London with as little attention to things around him, as if he were in a wilderness".

While in prayer he was lost in glorious absence. He seemed absorbed in God and the splendour which appeared on his countenance testified to this effect. Even when asleep the devotions of his conscious life continued to be activated.

He was a biblical genius and an amazing scholar. In addition to his mother tongue, Irish, he mastered English, Latin, Greek and Hebrew. The last of these gave him unparalleled delight".

"Oh truly laudable and worthy study, whereby a man is enabled to converse with God, with holy angels, with patriarchs and prophets, and clearly to unfold to men the mind of God from the language of God."

Each new hour of study was prefaced with petition in these words, "Lord Jesus, I lay my soul at Thy feet to be taught and governed by Thee. Take the veil from the mystery and show me the truth as it is in Thyself. Be Thou my sun and star by day and by night."

The venerable Wesley said of Walsh, "I knew a young man about twenty years ago, who was so thoroughly acquainted with the Bible, that if he was questioned concerning any Hebrew word in the Old or any Greek word in the New Testament, he would tell, after a little pause, not only how often the one or the other occurred in the Bible, but also what it meant in every place. His name was Thomas Walsh. Such a master of Bible knowledge I never saw before, and never expect to see again."

Here was both Irish saint and scholar united in one body. His zeal was as a flame of fire. People ran after him hungry for the words of grace that fell from his lips. Strong men were dissolved to tears. He preached on mountains and highways, meadows, private houses, prisons and ships.

So great was the success of his labours that the priests mobilised mobs to hound him from the towns and villages. He was verbally maligned, physically abused, beaten with sticks, pelted with stones.

Perhaps the most amazing element of Walsh's life is, that all this piety, education and trial is compressed into the short span of ten years. After suffering from a fevered illness, he passed away in the flower of life. He died at the age of twenty eight. His last but ecstacy-filled words were "He is come! He is come! My Beloved is mine, and I am His! His forever!"


## ADAM CLARKE

Ireland's greatest contribution to repaying its debt to the English Methodists was Adam Clarke. He was born in the Parish of Kilcronaghan near Maghera, in 1760. When about twelve years of age he came with his parents to reside in Ballyagherton midway between Coleraine and Portstewart.

After indulging in the usual activities of youth and manifesting evidences of intellectual brilliance, he heard the Methodist preachers. Before entering his twenties he found the Saviour. His zeal for the Lord captured the eye of John Wesley.

At twenty two years of age he went to England, hoping to

enter Kingswood school. Despite production of an introductory letter from Mr. Wesley, he was refused entrance. This was a bitter blow. He was penniless and only after earnest entreaty was he permitted a space in the brush and bucket room at the end of the Church.

He was so numbed with cold that he implored Mr. Simpson, the schoolmaster, to allow him to dig in the garden. He made a rich discovery that was to start him on his career as one of the greatest Oriental scholars in Europe at that time. He turned up a gold half sovereign. There were no claimants so Adam purchased a Hebrew Grammar by Cornelius Bailey!

In two weeks time he met Wesley who had returned to Bristol. Wesley commissioned him to the Bradford circuit where God used his youth and grace to lead many young people and older to the Saviour. He also won the affection of Mary Cooke who became his loving partner until the end of his brilliant life.

While labouring in the Norman Isles, now the Channel Isles, he gave himself relentlessly to study as well as his preaching vocation. He studied Greek, Latin, Hebrew, Chaldee, and Syriac.

## IN LABOURS MORE ABUNDANT

In 1789 Mr. Wesley felt that Adam Clarke should take supervision of the Dublin Society. This design did not materialise. Instead of going to Dublin he took charge of the Bristol Society. Despite ill health he gave himself to the care of a Society numbering two thousand people. He pursued his studies, and carried the organisational responsibilities of the 1790 Conference, which proved to be Mr. Wesley's last Conference appearance.

The succeeding years of his ministry were spent in Dublin, Manchester, Liverpool and London.

It was in the latter of these, as the century drew to its conclusion, that he began his immortal work now published in six volumes, "A Commentary on the Holy Scriptures."

He was, throughout life, wedded to his research and his pen. Translations of the Scripture in Syriac, Greek, Arabic and the Calmuc dialect; books on Persian, Hebrew and Greek grammars; the deciphering of the famous Rosetta stone which by its Coptic hieroglyphic language had baffled the linguists and antiquarians, were some of his achievements. He was also instrumental in producing the detailed "Memoirs of the Wesley Family." In 1808 he was awarded the Honorary Degree of Doctor of Law and Master of Arts, by Aberdeen University.

It was his great honour to dine with the most distinguished scholars in Europe at Kensington Palace by invitation of the Duke of Sussex. He was elected President of the British Conference three times, a unique honour only surpassed by Dr. Zabez Bunting after Dr. Clarke's decease.

He was also President of the Irish Conference four times.

He never lost the fervour of the simple Gospel preacher, and prevailed as a mighty soul-winner. What a testimony to the calibre of his spirituality!

## SUNSET AND SUNRISE

By the time he reached his seventieth year he was worn down. The church to which he had contributed such Herculean endeavours, mistreated him, but he persevered in spite of deep personal hurt. Two years later in 1832 he attended his final conference. He proceeded for home at Haydon Hall, calling with various relatives and friends on the way as well as preaching a few times.

He left home on Saturday 25 August 1832 to keep a preaching appointment at Bayswater the following Lord's Day. He was quite unwell that evening, and retired without taking supper.

Early next morning he arose, but it was with an earnest appeal to his hosts, Mr. and Mrs. Hobbs that he be taken home as quickly as possible. The request could not be fulfilled since he sank down a few moments later. He passed peacefully into the Lord's presence at eleven that evening.

He was laid to rest beside his one and only human hero - John Wesley.

Two churches stand in memory of his great ministry. One is in Portstewart, the other in Portrush. In front of the Portrush Church there is an obelisk. On one side these words are written, "In everlasting remembrance of Rev. Dr. Adam Clarke, natus circiter 1760, obut 1832. A servant of the Most High, who in preaching the Gospel with great labours and apostolic grace for more than fifty years, showed to myriads the way of salvation, and by his Commentaries on the Holy Scriptures, and other works of piety and learning yet speaks to passing generations. Soli Gloria Deo."

The other side reads "About the centenary of his birth, this obelisk, together with the Memorial Church at Portstewart, where he was brought up, has been erected by the subscriptions of the nobility, clergy, and the public at large of the British Islands, Canada and Australia A.D. 1859. Look reader at the Memorial and learn that youth consecrated to God, unswerving integrity of life, zeal for the common good, and diligent improvement of mind and talent, can raise the obscure to renown and immortality." Dr. Adam Clarke amply proved the validity of this inscription.

## OTHERS ALSO

Space does not permit us to consider the forty year ministry of Tipperary man Walter Griffith; William Arthur, author of "The Tongue of Fire" born in Kells 1819; the remarkable Irish preacher Gideon Ouseley who led multitudes of Roman Catholics to the Saviour; and William Thompson from Fermanagh who was first to occupy the Chair of Conference after John Wesley's death. Of these, and others from Ireland, Hulme makes reference to the striking tribute of Knox, "These are the men that can create a soul beneath the ribs of death."

## WHAT HATH GOD WROUGHT?

Only a little over half a century had elapsed since the

introduction of Methodism in Ireland. Wesley bade the people he loved a last farewell on July 12, 1789.

He sailed to the mainland leaving a legacy behind him. Eighty two Methodist chapels, sixty-five preachers, and about fourteen thousand members. One hundred and thirty-seven earnest devoted workers enlisted in the service of God.

The various churches of the land were leavened with the rich influences of the awakening. In process of time, these trusty followers of heart religion carried the message of the Gospel to France, Newfoundland, West Indies, Canada, and as already mentioned, America.

## TAKING ROOT IN SCOTLAND

It is not surprising that the genial influences of revival reached Scotland. The Spirit is not governed by the boundaries of men. Thus in July 1741 George Whitefield lifted up his voice in Edinburgh. Fitchett says that though Scotland had its good preachers, he excelled them all. "His deep melodious voice rang over vast crowds as with the vibrations of a great bell. The whole pathos, and passion, the rhetoric and visible tears running down his face just carried away the Scottish crowds".

In all he made fourteen visits, and preached to crowds of twenty thousand around Edinburgh. Butler in his work, "John Wesley and George Whitefield in Scotland," said "Whitefield moved the Scottish townspeople as Savanarola moved the populace of Florence in Italy".

His ministry reached its zenith at Cambuslang. The scenes could scarcely be described. People were weeping and falling into deep distress at eleven o'clock at night. Their agonies and cries pierced the air and prayer and praise could be heard all night. Sinners were slain in their scores. The sword of the Spirit pierced the heart; the effects of conviction travelled as swift as lightning.

Wesley followed Whitefield in 1751. While he never could subscribe to the Calvinistic theology which, in the main, prevailed in Scotland, he did minister with blessed success and no small amount of fruit. He loved the canny Scots as can be deduced from a total of twenty two visits. Citing Butler again he said that Wesley was, for Scotland, "a spiritual splendour."

The work may never have bulked large, but it takes its place among the branches of the work of God, and undoubtedly, there will be many, north of the border, among the celestial hosts who will bless God for the Methodist founder and his fellow-labourers.

## TAKING ROOT IN AMERICA

As before mentioned, American Methodism is traceable to a woman. Her name is Barbara Heck, and beside her stands Philip Embury and Captain Webb. The former two have been spoken of already. The latter was a great soldier of the 42nd Regiment who had been converted under Wesley's preaching at Bristol. He fought at the seige of Louisburg where he lost an eye due to a bullet wound. He was thought to be dead, but God raised him up to lead a small but heroic band of men in the defeat of General Wolfe. Thus France's grip on Canada was shattered.

Better still, he joined himself to the little band of Methodists at New York. He became a powerful preacher and an inspiration to the cause of Methodism in the New World.

Historians have concluded that, about the same time as Embury began to preach in his own house, Robert Strawbridge, who had also emigrated from County Leitrim, commenced preaching in the State of Maryland. This was at the beginning of 1766.

The first Methodist chapel was built and opened in 1768. Embury made its pulpit, being a carpenter by trade, and preached in it on October 30, of that year. The building itself measured sixty feet by forty-two feet. A fireplace and chimney adorned the room, thereby finding a loophole in the law which forbade any building of houses of worship other than Anglican.

The work grew quickly through the influx of other Methodist immigrants and the intriguing spectacle of Captain Webb preaching with great power in his full regimental dress.

With equal rapidity the work grew in Maryland. Robert Strawbridge built a log chapel in Sam's Creek. He laid two of his little children to rest beneath the rough pulpit. Wherever he went, he raised up preachers, and whenever he preached sinners were converted.

He also founded Methodism in the counties of Baltimore and Harford.

## THE MACEDONIAN CALL

Help was urgently required to maintain and extend the growing witness. Appeals were made to Mr. Wesley, but he took his own time to make a decision. Eventually in 1769 at the Leeds Conference Richard Boardman and Joseph Pilmoor volunteered to answer the call. Although they were the first officially appointed missionaries, they had been preceded by Robert Williams. When the appointed preacher arrived Williams went south with Pilmoor to Philadelphia, and also to Maryland later in association with Strawbridge.

He became the apostle of Methodism in Virginia and South Carolina. He was the first Methodist minister in America who published a book, the first to marry, the first that located and the first that died. At his funeral Francis Asbury said, "He has been a very useful laborious man; the Lord gave him many souls to his ministry."

## KEY EVENTS IN AMERICAN METHODISM

George Whitefield laid down his armour in 1771 after a life of abundant labours. In his wake there arrived one of the noblest men in early Methodism. His name is Francis Asbury.

## FRANCIS ASBURY

He was the son of a peasant household in Staffordshire. His preaching career commenced at the strippling age of seventeen years. Four years later he arrived as a probationer on the vast platform of American soil. His life and labours stand unparalleled in the first half-century of American Methodism. He was tall, thin, gaunt, but as tough as tempered steel; the steel of a super-human man and yet possessing the sweetest temper of a godly mother. Asbury was the apostle of perfect love and anointed prayer.

He travelled five thousand miles a year, often through shadowy untrodden forests, over wide prairies, across unbridged rivers. His total itinerary over forty five years is computed at two hundred and eighty thousand miles. He spent three hours a day in prayer, read a hundred pages of literature each day and mastered Latin, Greek and Hebrew.

Freeborn Garrettson said, "He prayed the best and prayed the most of all men I knew."

Francis Asbury carved a deeper niche in the social, moral and religious life of America than any other man either of his day or after it. He was the great file-leader of the evangelical cavalry that scoured the heights and depths of the new continent. Dr. Fitchett says the work grew with "almost tropical rapidity."

All this increased the work-load of the saintly Asbury. But he was an administrative genius! He knew his men. He knew where to place them. He knew how to suit the temper and genius of each preacher to each Society.

## THE CIVIL WAR

It was Francis Asbury who steered the church through the traumatic years of the civil war. Great man though Wesley was, he increased the difficulties for the infant work by his strong pro-British sympathies at the time. What was set forth as "A Calm Address to our American Colonies" became the source of great distress. Wesley's friends in America had to suppress the pamphlet there as much as possible, burning all the copies they could get their hands on.

Wesley's devotion to the Anglican church strained the loyalty of his people to breaking point in America as well as

England. If there were difficulties in finding ordained men to administer the sacraments before the war, they were much greater afterwards. They were widely dispersed before the conflict. As a result of it, those that had been in America mostly fled from the revolting colonies and abandoned their parishes.

The issue became urgent and of primary importance.

Wesley appealed to the Church of England to ordain some of his helpers. Not unexpectedly he received his reply in the negative.

## A TIME TO ORDAIN

During the next four years Wesley waited patiently. He implored Bishop Lowth of London twice who simply replied that there were three existent ordained men in America! Wesley replied that they were too few and in addition knew no more about saving souls than catching whales.

How providential it was in the long term as Wesley later observed, that his request was rejected! The people of America were now disengaged both from the State and the English hierarchy. If Wesley's men had been ordained they would still have been answerable to the Anglican bishops. Otherwise they were at liberty and Wesley appreciated the privileges.

What then was his course of action in the crisis of the day? Since there were no bishops with legal jurisdiction, and none to baptise or administer the Lord's Supper, Wesley felt he was invading no man's order or right by ordaining a man for the work.

## THOMAS COKE

In the company of his ordained friend Mr. Creighton, Wesley ordained Thomas Coke as a superintendent and Richard Whatcoat along with Thomas Vasey as presbyters for America. Coke was in turn, to ordain Asbury when he would arrive there.

Although Wesley ordained Dr. Coke as a superintendent, it

was really a play on terms occasioned by Wesley's rigidity to High Churchmanship. Coke was in all practical senses of the word a bishop, and this the American people saw sufficiently clearly to make the name and the office agree.

## A NEW CHURCH

At Christmas 1784, a few weeks after Dr. Coke's arrival, ministers and preachers gathered at Baltimore and by a unanimous vote Dr. Coke and Francis Asbury were elected as the first bishops of the Methodist Episcopal Church, whereupon Dr. Coke ordained Francis Asbury and also ordained a number of deacons and elders.

Thomas Coke was the great missionary-hearted man of eighteenth century Methodism. He often presided over the Irish and English Conferences after Wesley's death. He planted the witness in the West Indies among the Indian and German people of America, among the French, and died on his way, with six other missionaries, to establish the work in India. Dr. Matthew Simpson said, "No man in Methodism except Mr. Wesley, did more for the extension of the work through the world than did Dr. Coke."

## AMERICAN METHODISM

By virtue of its geographical and political environment, the daughter of Methodism gained her independence before the mother church in England. Within its first thirteen years from the arrival of Francis Asbury until his election as bishop in 1784 its membership had grown from five hundred to fifteen thousand, and that in spite of the civil war!

What an enviable record in the light of twentieth century advances! It was a revival church in its spirit and a missionary church in its organization. People were added to it, not in hundreds, but in thousands.

Joshua Marsden wrote in 1802 his impressions of the work. He describes the plainness of the preachers, their total dedication to missions, and their success, "In England,

Methodism is like a river calmly gliding on; here it is a torrent rushing along, and sweeping all away in its course."

Within the ministry of Francis Asbury and under his leadership the Methodist movement developed from fourteen itinerant preachers with three hundred and seventy-one members, to seven hundred itinerants, two thousand local preachers and two hundred and fourteen thousand members.

Those who wish to read further concerning the great work of God in those days will find deep inspiration and challenge through that renowned work of Abel Stephens, the excellent historian of Methodism.

## THE LIGHT SHINES ON

During the course of these chapters we have briefly sketched the advance of Methodism from those first beginnings in 1739 during its first sixty years, or thereabouts. No single work can do justice to the full pageant of this movement. The heroism, the administration, the transforming work on nations and individuals will only shine in their full splendour in eternity.

A few individuals have been identified not because they were possessed of any superior spirituality but because God in his grace saw them as fit channels for leadership. Scores of others, though lesser known, take their place in the role of honour.

"Through faith (they) subdued kingdoms, wrought righteousness, obtained promises, stopped the mouths of lions, quenched the violence of fire, escaped the edge of the sword, out of weakness were made strong, waxed valiant in fight, turned to flight the armies of the aliens . . . and others were tortured not accepting deliverance . . . others had trial of cruel mockings and scourgings, yea moreover of bonds and imprisonment. They were stoned, they were sawn asunder, were tempted, were slain with the sword . . . These all obtained a good report through faith . . . "Hebrews 11 v 33-39."

This great scriptural record of the historic worthies bears so many striking resemblances in the lives of the early Methodists.

They have passed on to their abundant reward. Wesley himself crossed the river on March 2, 1791. His immortal phrase, "The best of all is, God is with us," resounds from the death chamber of the great saint. He left a legacy in terms of a great movement, a scholarly library of some two hundred and thirty three volumes, and an army of almost three hundred preachers to carry the torch into the next century.

He went aloft with the benedictions of more than one hundred and twenty thousand souls on earth and swept through the pearly gates to the hosannas of thousands who had preceded him.

But Methodism was not to die with Wesley. One century after its formation as a church in America the Methodist Episcopal Church North had a total of over one million members and during the next four years to 1870 added another two hundred thousand.

The passing of time is the severest critic of every religious movement. Rarely does a movement outlast its first generation. Its primary thrust becomes a spent force and by the law of averages, founders generally pass through the agony of seeing their work beginning to languish. The remarkable thing about Methodism is the sustained energy it possessed throughout the greater part of Wesley's life.

True, it has had its fragmentations, the first within seven years of Wesley's death but Fitchett declared "the spiritual impulse of true Methodism has survived all its schisms."

God has not, nor ever will, leave himself without a witness to the message and fervour which stirred England and America in the eighteenth century.

# 8

# THE PREDOMINANT TEACHINGS OF THE AWAKENING

When an individual reflects on the great Methodist awakening of the eighteenth century, some recognition must be given to the kernel of the message declared. The Wesleyan revival has some very clearly defined distinctives which have already been alluded to. The universality of sin and the possibility of salvation for all men figured prominently in the revival. The doctrine of assurance occasioned great opposition. To give expression to, or experience of, religion by which a man could know he was forgiven and be assured of salvation was presumptive to the highest degree. But these were the truths that men most required, and by the grace of God through Whitefield and Wesley they heard them. Multitudes were moved by what they heard, and found a gracious God, disposed to pardon, and adopt them as His children.

To all these aspects of truth Wesley gave his heart and energy. In addition to these, the Wesleys carried a great burden and a burning conviction regarding holiness. John Wesley was not content to leave a justified sinner with the idea that he had arrived in the spiritual race.

The Wesleyan reformation was a reform to holiness.

Methodism was, from its inception, even in Oxford, a movement in pursuit of heart purity.

Wesley himself was under no illusions as to why God had brought about the movement of which he became the figure head. In a letter dated September 15, 1790, six months before his death, he wrote to his friend, Mr. Robert Brackenbury. In the central paragraph he said, "I am glad brother, O . . . has more light with regard to full sanctification. This doctrine is the grand depositum which God has lodged with the people called Methodists; and for the sake of propagating this chiefly. He appears to have raised them up".

The neglect of this message was an unforgiveable omission in any lay preacher's ministry, and was dealt with quite drastically.

At the advanced age of eighty-seven, Wesley was unequivocal in his language. The following letter to Dr. Adam Clarke bears this out.

London, November 26, 1790

Dear Adam, To retain the grace of God is much more than to gain it; hardly one in three does this. And this should be strongly and explicitly urged on all who have tasted perfect love. If we can prove that any of our local preachers or leaders, either directly or indirectly speak against it, let him to be a local preacher or leader no longer. I doubt whether he should continue in Society, because he that could speak thus in our congregations could not be an honest man . . .

Wesley's doctrine of holiness has been the subject of much consideration, both for and against. It was the occasion of much offence during his lifetime, and evoked strong opposition on the part of many. To preach it, as Wesley did, exposed one to the charge of being worse than a heathen or a publican.

Nevertheless he pursued his track without intermission and gave his utmost energy to spreading the message of holiness over these lands.

Beneficially, for succeeding generations, Wesley was a prolific writer. A legacy of publications is readily available, in which all that Wesley declared, relative to this issue, is open to scrutiny. His successors, both friend and foe, have ample foundational material upon which to build their conclusions.

The chief source of Wesley's doctrine is his oft-revised book, "A Plain Account of Christian Perfection."

Equally explicit are his sermons on the subject, along with many references in his Journals and Letters. His brother, Charles, gave poetic style to the doctrine in his hymnology.

What was it which led Wesley to embrace this position in the first place?

## HIS EARLY IMPRESSIONS

Interestingly his perceptions were being formed previous to his conversion. To him, holiness was an intrinsic element of salvation.

Question:- What was the rise of Methodism, so called?

Answer:- In 1729 two young men searching the Bible saw they could not be saved without holiness, followed after it and incited others so to do. In 1737 they saw holiness comes by faith. They saw likewise that men are justified before they are sanctified but still holiness was their point. God then thrust them out, utterly against their will to raise up a holy people.

Wesley did in effect preach in this vein at St. Mary's Church, Oxford on January 1, 1733. His subject was "The Circumcision of the Heart." His introductory remarks are indicative of his spiritual perceptions at this point in his life.

"It is that habitual disposition of the soul, which in the sacred writings is termed holiness, and which implies the being cleansed from sin; from all filthiness both of flesh and spirit; and by consequence, the being endued with those virtues which were in Christ Jesus; the being so renewed in the image of our mind as to be perfect as our Father in Heaven is perfect".

Arvid Gradin, the Moravian, was the first to define "the full assurance of faith" to a seeking Wesley, three months after his conversion experience.

"Repose in the blood of Christ; a firm confidence in God, and persuasion of His favour; the highest tranquility, serenity and peace of mind with a deliverance from all fleshly desire, and a cessation from all, even inward sins".

After conversion there are various references to his true heart perceptions. "I believe justification to be wholly distinct from sanctification and necessarily antecedent to it. September 13, 1739."

## THE DOCTRINE DEFINED

The next twenty years in particular, and throughout the remainder of his life in general, Wesley expressed, defined and qualified the word and terminology. His first tract on Christian Perfection was published in 1739. He entitled it "The Character of a Methodist", and outlined the life of a perfect Christian.

"He loves God with all his heart, with all his soul, with all his mind and, with all his strength . . . In everything giveth thanks as knowing this (whatsoever it is) is the will of God in Christ Jesus concerning him . . . He prays without ceasing . . . His heart is lifted up to God at all times, and in all places. Loving God he loves his neighbour as himself; He loves every man as his own soul. He loves his enemies, yea, and the enemies of God . . . He is pure in heart. Love has purified his heart from envy, malice, wrath and every unkind temper. As he loves God, so he keeps his commandments . . . Whatever God has forbidden he avoids. Whatsoever he doeth is all to the Glory of God. Nor do the customs of the world at all hinder him from running the race which is set before. Whatsoever things are pure, whatsoever things are lovely . . . he thinks, spends and acts, adorning the doctrine of God our Saviour in all things".

This positive element of an unrivalled love for God in the heart and life was the vital dimension of Wesley's message. It was more than a doctrine to be declared; it was a life to be lived and an experience to be enjoyed.

Although the term Christian Perfection was the most

employed synonym for the message, Wesley's favourite couplet was 'perfect love.'

It was this message which marked the preachers of the movement. Three elements are worthy of brief consideration in this effective doctrine of Methodism.

## A. AN INSTANTANEOUS BLESSING

It is on this point many took issue with Wesley. For them, salvation or sanctification was a gradual process progressing throughout life until death becomes the great deliverer.

There are some questions requiring clarification. Did Wesley define the entrance of perfect love as momentary? What provoked him to do so? How, or when, did he arrive at this conclusion? Did he insist on this strongly?

All the evidences point to "an instantaneous blessing," although, as Cox observes, "At first Wesley was not certain whether this entire sanctification was obtained gradually or instantaneously."

A short resume of his various records and statements show how quickly his perceptions were formed. The earlier years tended to the more gradual development leading to the crisis moment but particularly from 1760, the instantaneous aspect gained the ascendancy.

In 1744, at the first Methodist Conference, it was stated, "When we begin to believe, then sanctification begins, and as faith increases, holiness increases, till we are created anew."

By 1749 a very definite statement was manifest, (1) Christian Perfection . . . implies deliverance from sin. (2) This is received merely by faith. (3) That it is given instantaneously, in one moment. (4) That we are to expect it every moment; now is the accepted time, now is the day of salvation.

In 1761 there were still few witnesses to the blessing. What was the reason? "We sought it by our works; we thought it was to come gradually; we never expected it to come in a moment by simple faith, in the very same manner as we received justification."

In his sermons he constantly stresses the vitality of present faith for the blessing.

"The doctrine of Christian perfection attainable in an instant by a simple act of faith, was made prominent in Methodist congregations in 1762, and ever after it was one of the chief topics of Mr. Wesley's ministry and that of itinerant preachers, according to Dr. Tyerman".

When he wrote to Charles, his brother, in 1766, he urged him, "Insist everywhere on full redemption received now by faith alone . . . Press the instantaneous blessing."

It is obvious that Wesley's strong point for instant deliverance lay in the conditional cause, namely, faith. If the blessing was obtainable by faith, then why not exercise faith now? Faith can release the blessing in a moment, whereas works can never achieve it. He said, "You think I must be or do thus or thus. Then you are seeking it by works unto this day. If you are seeking it by faith, you may expect it as you are now; . . It is of importance to observe that there is an inseparable connection between these three points, expect it by faith, expect it as you are, expect it now! To deny one of them is to deny them all . . ."

Wesley not only pressed the instantaneous blessing on the promise of it being an inheritance of faith, but on the basis of multiplied testimonies and carefully sifted evidence from the lives of those who enjoyed it.

The widespread and simultaneous phenomena stirred Wesley. In Bristol, Kingswood and London, not forgetting Ireland, men and women were standing forth, presenting a crystal-clear testimony to instantaneous full deliverance from sin. In London alone, at the beginning of the 1760's, Wesley found six hundred and fifty-two members of the Society who enjoyed a sky-blue experience of heart holiness - something even the exacting scrutiny of Wesley could not discount. This work continued in the succeeding years with great and widespread effect.

Wesley writes, "Everyone of these . . . has declared his deliverance from sin was instantaneous; that the change was wrought in a moment. Had half of these or one-third, or even one in twenty declared it was gradually wrought on them, I should have believed this, with regard to them and thought that some were gradually sanctified and some instantaneously. But as I have not found in so long a space of time, a single person speaking thus . . . I cannot but believe that sanctification is commonly, if not always, an instantaneous work."

## B. AN ASSURED BLESSING

The blessed doctrine of assurance, with its attendant expression in testimony, was the striking characteristic of Methodism. In his Plain Account, Wesley proceeds to make a point of the reality and necessity of assurance or the witness of the Spirit to perfect love.

In some measure he advocated caution with regard to testifying to the experience. For instance, when asked, Question:- Suppose one had attained to this would you advise him to speak of it?

Answer:- At first, perhaps, he would scarce be able to refrain, the fire would be so hot within him; his desire to declare the loving kindness of the Lord carrying him away like a torrent. But afterwards he might: and then it would be advisable not to speak of it to them that know not God . . . nor to others, without some particular reason, without some good in view. And then he should have especial care to avoid the appearance of boasting; to speak with the deepest humility and reverence giving all the glory to God.

Bearing in mind these cautionary words of advice from Mr. Wesley let us note his emphasis on assurance.

Question:- But how do you know that you are sanctified, saved from your inbred corruption?

Answer:- I can know it no otherwise than I know that I am justified. "Hereby know we that we are of God," in either sense, "by the Spirit that He hath given us."

This clear, unequivocal response was one of the foundation proofs Wesley employed on various occasions. He was prepared to make the admission that sometimes the witness was not so lucid as at other times, but then again is the same premise not applicable to the matter of justification? Less or more, there is a striking parallelism.

As to his utterance regarding others, he said, "None therefore ought to believe that the work is done till there is added the testimony of the Spirit witnessing his entire sanctification as clearly as his justification."

Far be it from one to query Wesley's judgement here, but rather admire his caution and sincerity, but it is also true to life that the witness often comes at the moment of confession. At least, this is so relative to justification and known by one personally to be factually so relative to entire sanctification. "If thou shalt confess with thy mouth ... and shalt believe in thine heart ... thou shalt be saved." Romans 10 v 9. However, on the point at issue, Wesley was just as explicit that a person could be entirely sanctified and know it as he could be justified and know it.

On occasions, Wesley determined to sift the evidence and test the experience of certain individuals. "Having desired that as many as could of the neighbouring towns, who believed that they were saved from sin, would meet me, I spent the greatest part of the day in examining them one by one. The testimony of some I could not receive; but concerning the far greatest part, it is plain (unless they could be supposed to tell wilful and deliberate lies). (1) That they feel no inward sin, and to the best of their knowledge, commit no outward sin. (2) That they see and love God every moment, and pray, rejoice and give thanks evermore. (3) That they have constantly as clear a witness from God of sanctification as they have of justification. Now in this do I rejoice, call it what you please."

"Dr. R. Newton Flew was sceptical about Wesley's doctrine of assurance relative to entire sanctification. "While a man may bear testimony to his awareness of a God who is able to destroy the last remains of sin, he cannot know himself well enough to claim that God has actually done the work. The very sense of feeling that one has left a permanently low plane of "spiritual experience and is now on a permanently higher plane smacks of pride."

Indeed, it is very valid to express this feeling. The extent of a man's purity may be no more than the extent of his awareness of sinfulness, which in certain cases may be limited. But then, Wesley was careful to qualify the basis and conditions before he would accept at face value a person's statements. Furthermore, it is a misplaced emphasis to trust in a subjective experience. It is true that man cannot know himself well enough, but the assurance is the fruit of an objective trust; the voice of God. It is the witness borne to the soul by the Holy Ghost alone which provided a reliable basis for a full and blessed testimony.

## C. AN EMPHASISED MESSAGE

In keeping with the topic of our subject, namely, the emphasis, we conclude with some account of the measure with which Wesley enforced the message. The first four Conferences of Methodism 1744-1747 gave serious consideration to the doctrine and declaration of full salvation.

When Wesley wrote to Freeborn Garrettson in 1785, he said, "The more explicitly and strongly you press all believers to aspire after full sanctification, as attainable now by simple faith, the more the whole work of God will prosper."

As we have already noted in his letter of Mr. Brackenbury (1790), Wesley saw this message as the "grand depositum, and for the sake of propogating this chiefly, He (God) appeared to have raised Methodism up."

If the work was languishing in any area, Wesley believed it resulted from a neglect of this message. "I was surprised to find fifty members fewer than I left in it last October. One reason is Christian Perfection has been little insisted on; and wherever this is not done, be the preachers ever so elequent, there is little increase, either in the number or grace of the hearers."

Thus we have in some small way traced the message which was the marrow of Methodism: the doctrine and experience of Christian Perfection, as Wesley defined and declared it. One is brought back again and again to his positive emphasis, namely, the loving of God with all the heart and one's neighbour as oneself. He did not so much set out to formulate a doctrine but to present a manner of life and living. To him, it was not a new message, but a rediscovery of Biblical experience. Between the extremes of Augustinianism on one hand, and Pelagianism on the other hand, Wesley found a balance. Human freedom enabled by Divine and necessary grace, restored the equilibrium to the message of his day and resulted in one of the greatest awakenings ever experienced on the English mainland.

Throughout his protracted quest for holiness, he never allowed himself to be diverted. How influential were those early encounters with the mystics Law, Scougal and Taylor. How providential his acquaintance with the Moravians. Often, as a solitary figure, he moved irresistibly forward to spread scriptural holiness over these lands and, in time, became the commander-in-chief of a great army dedicated to the message of Perfect Love.

# 9

# NEW VOICES AFTER WESLEY

Throughout Wesley's lifetime the Methodist cause, in England at least, maintained its unity. This was due, in greater part, to the authority Wesley imposed by his strong leadership. Any semblance of dissension was over-ridden by the greater organisational structure of the movement. Wesley himself took great satisfaction in the unity of his work. "The Methodists are one . . . though mountains rise and oceans roll to sever us in vain."

But the seed-bed for change was present in spite of Wesley's controlling power. The Established Church had little sympathy for Wesley's people. It had lesser identity on the spiritual level. Could a humble godly people, anxious for the administration of the sacraments and the benefits of the church, be expected to subscribe to such a paradox indefinitely? Were their own preachers never to obtain the right to administer the sacraments?

It was too much to expect, and the expected transpired.

## ENGLISH METHODISM
## THE PLAN OF PACIFICATION

This was introduced in 1795. Responsiblity was placed upon the individual Societies. They must decide if they supported the reading of the liturgy, or at least Wesley's abridgment of it, and the lessons of the Calendar during established church service hours. Would they support the administration of the sacrament by certain persons authorised by the Conference? The decision was supported by all but six preachers who refused to sign a declaration of voluntary adhesion to the Large Minutes. This overwhelming support for the plan signified the separate identities of the two bodies.

Though the final break took many years to fully effect, Methodism had established itself as a fledgling denomination. It should be said that provision was made for those who wished to continue in the former association, and many did, such was the loyalty to the parent church.

## THE METHODIST NEW CONNEXION

Alexander Kilham, along with William Thorn and four others, refused to accept the plan of Pacification. He was a reformer, and really in advance of his time. For him the plan did not go far enough. He pressed ardently for greater laity involvement in the governing of church affairs. He attacked his fellow-preachers, terming the government popery and priestcraft. He was called to substantiate his accusations, but on failure to do so he was expelled in 1796.

It is unfortunate that the impending breach could not be avoided, but there we must leave the matter. The following year the new body was officially identified as the New Connexion with an enrolment of five thousand members.

It had its counterpart in Ireland at the same time, for thirty-two preachers on the Lisburn circuit were expelled for advocating similar views. Both bodies formed an association.

Kilham was a fervent young preacher who gave himself enthusiastically to his new work. We are never to know what might have been accomplished through his life since he died suddenly in 1798 at the youthful age of thirty six years.

## PRIMITIVE METHODISTS

There is much that could be written of this body. It became the second largest Methodist body to the parent Wesleyan church. It experienced rapid growth and prosperity. It enjoyed constant extension although it drew but a small number of adherents from the main body.

Some very informative accounts of its work among the unchurched and neglected people are in existence. One of these is 'The Romance of Primitive Methodism' by Joseph Ritson.

The founder, Hugh Bourne was born in 1772 in Staffordshire. He became an active preacher in the Wesleyan Methodist Church, having been wonderfully converted in 1799.

He was instrumental in the salvation of quite a godless character called Daniel Shubotham on Christmas Day 1800. He, in turn, won Matthias Bayley to the Saviour. These men were new to a new world, but God began to use them, through conversation evangelism and prayer meetings. Their activities were centred around Mow Cop, an area about three miles north-west of Bemersley and situated 1091 feet above sea level at the south western point of the Pennines.

He preached his first sermon on July 12, 1801 in the open-air at Joseph Pointon's house due to a large crowd having gathered to hear the shy but much loved talker of salvation. He was so bashful that he couldn't look at his great congregation and he held his hand over his face as a type of screen, somewhat like a very small child is accustomed to do in the presence of strangers.

But God saved a soul and that gave him courage to continue.

Amongst all those who were finding the Saviour there was one who was to prove an invaluable and trusted co-partner in this revival movement. His name was Willam Clowes. After a profligate life he was saved on 20 January 1805.

He made a clear break with his former life and associations and opened his home for the religious services. He became an effective soul-winner although the Methodist Church was loathe to licence him as a preacher.

There was no desire at this stage to establish a new denomination, but the succeeding five years saw a widening gap between the two parties.

## CAMP MEETING EVANGELISM

Lorenzo Dow, an eccentric but dynamic soul-winner who had laboured in the Methodist work in America appeared on the English scene. His reports of the great camp-meetings in America fired the enthusiasm of Hugh Bourne. Consequently on 31 May 1807 Mow Cop was crowded with a vast host of people. Stands were erected and preachers exhorted the people to repentance. Much fruit was gathered into the garner. It was the first of many and the great distinctive arm of the Primitive evangelistic labour throughout the century.

It was just such a practice which drew the fire of the mainline Methodists. The issue was brought before the 1807 Conference. The judgment was given that even though they were allowable means of evangelism in America, they were highly improper in England and likely to produce considerable mischief.

The leaders were somewhat discouraged, but they proceeded to hold another meeting in August. The hand of the Lord was outstretched again in blessing. This was all that Bourne and his accomplices needed. Their course was being firmly set. They would obey God rather than man.

Hugh Bourne was formally expelled from the Methodist Society of Burslem on 27 June 1808.

During 1809 Bourne and Clowes developed a closer co-operation in the work. The former gave up secular work at the clear call of God and stepped out in naked faith.


## A NEW DENOMINATION

The labours of these two men extended. Societies were born out of their successes. Class tickets were printed for May 1811. It was the start of a new but yet nameless work. That was settled in February 1812. It would be Primitive Methodist.

These men had laboured toward the restoration of that primitive zeal which they saw in Wesley and Whitefield's ministry. Unfortunately the parent body failed to give them the recognition they deserved.

There was no secession of members from the Wesleyans; no split with the mother church. The Primitives started off on clear ground. They withdrew from the places of Methodist appointment and before long established thirteen new centres increasing their membership from ten to one hundred and thirty six. The work started from fundamental basics in every way.

## LATER ADVANCES

Though it is not within the scope of this work to furnish a detailed history of the movement, it is of interest to note its progress.

Lady evangelists were very prominent in its progress. God used their ministry in very effective ways.

Laity were given an important role in the decision making processes of the movement.

It had by 1853 in Great Britain, a period of forty years after its inception, one thousand seven hundred and eighty nine chapels, over three and a half thousand preaching places, five hundred and sixty eight travelling and over nine and a half thousand local preachers, and six thousand seven hundred and sixty seven class leaders. By 1859 it had almost one hundred and twenty three thousand members.

It formed a missionary movement in 1843 and established in Australia, Africa, America, Canada and various other mission fields. Bourne himself could not have foreseen the end product of his course, but it can only be accounted in the light of the divine pattern. "He takes the weak things of the world, to confound the things which are mighty".

## THE BIBLE CHRISTIAN METHODISTS

William O'Bryan was born in Devon in 1778. He had the rare privilege as a boy of being prayed for by John Wesley. The ageing father of Methodism placed his hand on his head, uttering words that were both an inspiration and a prophecy, "May he be a blessing to hundreds and to thousands."

He found the Saviour in 1795 and became zealous for the salvation of his neighbours. He was a young man full of devotion. Prayer and fasting were deeply wrought into his life. He first preached in 1801 and felt clearly called to this work seven years later. His ardour for winning the lost took him wherever he was invited. Some fellow preachers disapproved of his itinerations and by 1810 he was expelled from the Methodists, without trial or defence. Between the years 1810 and 1814 he established a number of Societies until he was induced to rejoin the parent church along with his Societies in 1814. The reconciliation was short-lived as he was excluded from the local society for missing class meetings over three weeks.

O'Bryan was a courteous man, approaching the clergy before preaching in their parishes. He was not, however, to be silenced by their non-consent.

The first separate society was formed in 1815, and subsequently, the first chapel was built, and opened at Shebbear, which became a focal centre of the denomination.

## HEROIC LABOURS

At the first quarterly meeting in January 1816 two hundred and thirty seven members were reported. Fifteen months later there were almost one thousand more added to the work.

Within a few years the work had reached Cornwall, Isle of Wight, Kent, and Northumberland.

Godly women pioneers were wooing the lost in London to the Saviour.

By 1819 there were thirty travelling preachers, sixteen of them being women and by 1823, one hundred women were labouring as preachers, local or itinerant.

Johanna Neale, led hundreds to the Saviour in Devon. Mary Toms planted the flag in the Isle of Wight and Mary Werrey wrought a great and lasting work in the Channel Isles in spite of opposition. In nine months she preached on average ten times each week, secured one hundred and forty one class meeting members and the erection of a chapel. Afterwards she pioneered the work in Northumberland.

William O'Bryan also carried the gospel to Canada in the 1830's. He lived to the great age of ninety years and passed away in 1868.

It must have been extremely gratifying to the founder to find they had gained a total membership of fourteen and a half thousand people by 1842. The missionary arm, for which the work was noted had already reached Australasia and the English-speaking peoples of Canada.

# UNITED METHODIST FREE CHURCHES

The thirty years between 1827-1857 saw a number of schisms within Methodism. The Protestant Methodists were formed in 1827. Conference supported a call for the erection of an organ in Brunswick Wesleyan Chapel in Leeds. In so doing it over-ruled the district meeting's decision.

The leading antagonist was Matthew Johnston who was subsequently suspended from the local preacher's office. Seventy Leeds preachers supported him and ceased their labours. Ministerial supremacy prevailed, the organ was installed at the cost of one thousand pounds and one thousand members. The ramifications of this high handed action on the part of Conference spread as far as London. Where might this authoritarian approach appear next?

It was the conflict between conference and a section of the Manchester circuit which led to the eventual formation of the Wesleyan Methodist Association. The focus of conflict was the proposed establishment of a theological institution for the training of young preachers. It was viewed with alarm. This would take away the individuality, variety and force of the founding fathers of Methodism. There seemed to be no reconciliation of the divergent views, thus it was that in 1836 the new body appeared. It fully subscribed to Methodist doctrines, ordinances and institutions, while giving independence in circuit and church affairs. Its Assembly was freely elected by the circuits from both ministers and laymen, the number sent being proportionate to the membership of each circuit.

The Association grew by accretion at first. About eight thousand members were expelled or seceded from the Methodist Church. In 1836 it was strengthened by the amalgamation of the Protestant Methodists and the Independent Methodists from Scarborough. To these we must also add the Arminian Methodists from Derby, a fellowship of six hundred members and four local preachers who had suffered expulsion in 1831.

By 1839 the Association had twenty eight thousand members and six hundred chapels. This Association continued until 1857 when by its union with the Wesleyan Reformer, the body known as the United Methodist Free Churches was formed. The combined membership was almost forty thousand people, one hundred and ten preachers, and seven hundred and sixty nine chapels. Within five years membership had increased by a further twenty thousand due to aggressive evangelistic efforts. One of those who effected a remarkable ministry in the movement was the notable James Caughey.

It was the beginning of the twentieth century, 1907 which saw the amalgamation of the Bible Christian Methodists, the Methodist New Connexion and the United Methodist Free Churches. The union was legalised in The United Methodist Church Act 1907. The Primitive Methodist Church and the Independent Methodist Churches maintained their separate identities.

In this brief resume we have glanced at the more major events within English Methodism during the nineteenth century. Whether one feels the various sessions and divisions were justified, or could on the other hand have been prevented, the obvious result was the maintenance of the old-time message, at least by a remnant.

## AMERICAN METHODISM
The Church in America was governed by the Conference

both annual and General. This was composed more and more of the clerical order. Power to direct lay with the bishops, Francis Asbury being the foremost. Though the great mass of work was being effected by circuit riders, and an army of anointed lay-preachers, they had no authoritative voice at the governing level of the church. From time to time, during the first quarter of the nineteenth century pamphlets appeared and lobby groups were formed to campaign on these men's behalf. But it was a prejudice which could not easily be overthrown.

## METHODIST PROTESTANT CHURCH

Eventually a large convention convened in Baltimore and the first off-shoot was formed.

Episcopacy was retained but laymen were immediately introduced into all the legislative work of the denomination. When founded in 1830 it was composed of one hundred and fourteen ministerial and lay delegates representing about five thousand members.

When the denomination met for the first General Conference in 1834 it had five hundred preachers and almost twenty seven thousand members! This was surely a remarkable addition: twenty two thousand people in four years!

Overtures were made by the Episcopal church with a view to re-uniting the two bodies. After some lengthy discussions, and a formation of a basis for reunion the matter was resolved at Baltimore on May 16, 1877, thus annexing a total of fifty eight thousand people to the parent church again.

## SLAVERY

The Methodist Episcopal Church was not disposed to taking a stand against the widespread practice of slave-labour. In the 1840's two new bodies made their appearance on this issue. The Wesleyan Methodist Church of America was founded in New York in 1843. This Northern body abolished episcopacy, introduced laymen to its governing structures and lifted up a higher spiritual and ethical standard among its people.

Its prohibition extended beyond slavery, to the membership of secret societies and worldly fashion. It sought to bring its people back to early Wesleyan ideals. The reaction by the parent church to the Wesleyan Methodist position drove a wedge betwen its own denomination north and south. As a result the Methodist Episcopal Church South was born in Louisville on May 1, 1845.

After legal proceedings, property was transferred to the Southern body. At the time of separation there were about half a million members in the Southern Church. Fifteen years later this figure had increased to seven hundred and fifty seven thousand.

After the civil war in the 1860's many of the coloured people formed the African Methodist Episcopal Church.

## FREE METHODIST CHURCH

One can see that secessions in Methodism did not take place, in general, on doctrinal differences. The Wesleyan Methodists did charge the mainline church with some doctrinal looseness. This was also the case with the establishment of Free Methodism.

In the Genesee Conference in Western New York, the establishment was controlled by men who were mostly members of a secret order, and who discriminated against the old-school Methodists.

Benjamin T. Roberts took the brunt of an unfair trial by the Conference at its highest level. His expulsion caused widespread indignation in Western New York and in other parts also.

The result was the formation of the Free Methodist Church in 1860.

Some of the pertinent issues, were the re-establishment of a strong emphasis on Wesleyan holiness teaching, the requirement that members assert belief in the doctrine of entire sanctification; plainness of dress, and the abolition of the rented pew system. This latter meant equal privileges for all members, not just the wealthy few.

Though it never became a very large movement, it established missionary outreach work and has built its Societies in Europe, Canada, South America, Africa and the Far East. It continues to exist and carry on its witness within the world-wide Methodist bodies.

In addition to these early and main divisions in the Methodist movement, there are many smaller associations in existence throughout America.

Some account for a membership of a few hundred while the majority have between two and ten thousand people in fellowship.

## CONCLUDING SUMMARY

World Methodism stands two hundred and fifty years further along the road of time, since John Wesley's heart was strangely warmed. Throughout its long history the name of Wesley has been held in highest honour. But allegiance to the founder's name does not insure allegiance to his fundamental beliefs. Days of doctrinal decline and modernistic tendencies have eaten at the heart of many older Methodist bodies.

The pattern of history is, that when a body forfeits its trust, the Spirit of God raises up a people, usually from its own ranks, who perpetuate the message in a new association or denomination.

The striking factor in our consideration of these various branches of methodism has been the issues which led to their formation. Some would consider them unjustifiable. Yet, those same denominations experienced some remarkable growth.

Tens of thousands were reached through their witness. Evidently the Spirit of God can bring good out of that which is often considered evil and unnecessary. His willingness to employ and maintain the witness of those who may be disdained by men is a constant source of inspiration. Thus they press on with vigour, supported by the conviction of a clear conscience and a sense of loyalty to the truths delivered by the greatest figure in eighteenth century England - John Wesley.

"Let earth and heaven agree,
Angels and men be joined,
To celebrate with me
The Saviour of mankind;
To adore the all-atoning Lamb,
And bless the sound of Jesu's Name".

"Oh for a trumpet voice,
On all the world to call,
To bid their hearts rejoice
In Him who died for all;
For all my Lord was crucified,
For all, for all my Saviour died".